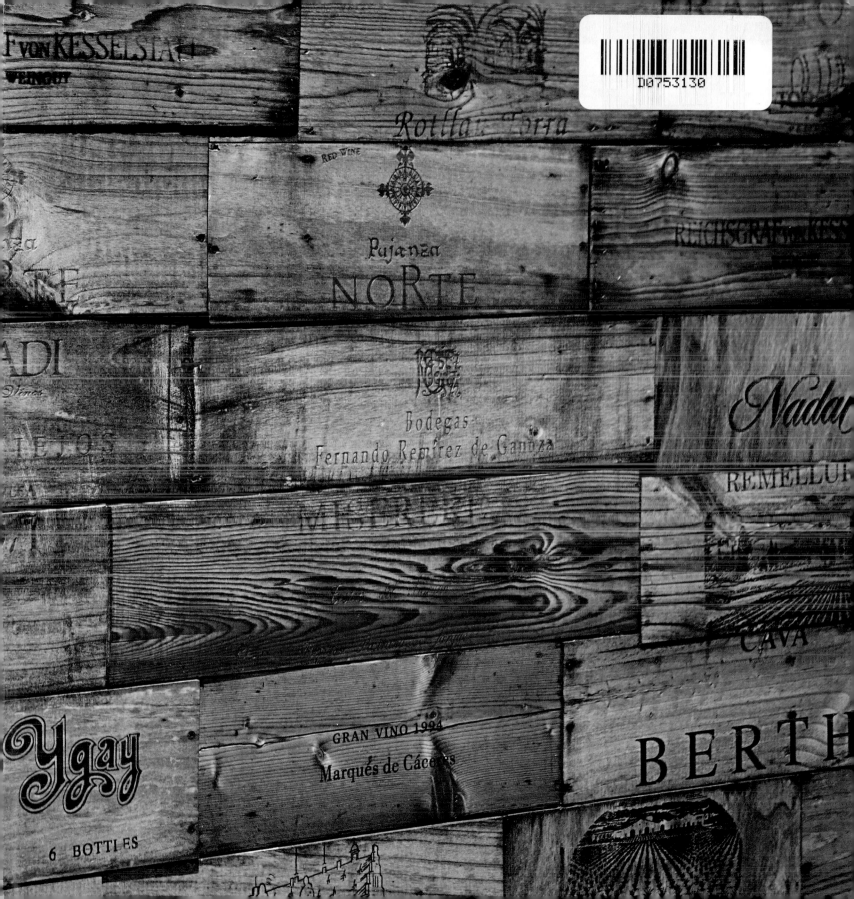

THE DESSERTS OF JORDI ROCA

THE DESSERTS OF JORDI ROCA

OVER 80 DESSERT RECIPES CONCEIVED IN EL CELLER DE CAN ROCA

PETER PAUPER PRESS, INC.
White Plains, New York

The Desserts of Jordi Roca

First published in Spain under the title *Los Postres de Jordi Roca*
© Jordi Roca, 2011
© Photographs: Becky Lawton, 2011

Props Styling: Agnes Cobotaite
Post Production: Bjorn Badetti
Design and cover: Jordi Galeano
Edition: Pere Romanillos
Prepress: Aura Digit
Edited by Esther Sanz

Original edition copyright © EDITORIAL OCÉANO, S.L., Barcelona, Spain
English translation copyright © 2015 Peter Pauper Press, Inc.
First published in English in 2015 by Peter Pauper Press, Inc.

Published by Peter Pauper Press, Inc.
202 Mamaroneck Avenue
White Plains, New York 10601
U.S.A.

Published in the United Kingdom and Europe by
Peter Pauper Press, Inc.
c/o White Pebble International
Unit 2, Plot 11 Terminus Road
Chichester, West Sussex PO19 8TX, UK

Library of Congress Cataloging-in-Publication Data Available

ISBN 978-1-4413-0856-6
Manufactured for Peter Pauper Press, Inc.
Printed in Hong Kong
7 6 5 4 3 2 1

Visit us at www.peterpauper.com

To my parents, brothers, and the great family of El Celler de Can Roca.
But most especially to you, who is holding this in your hands.

Summary

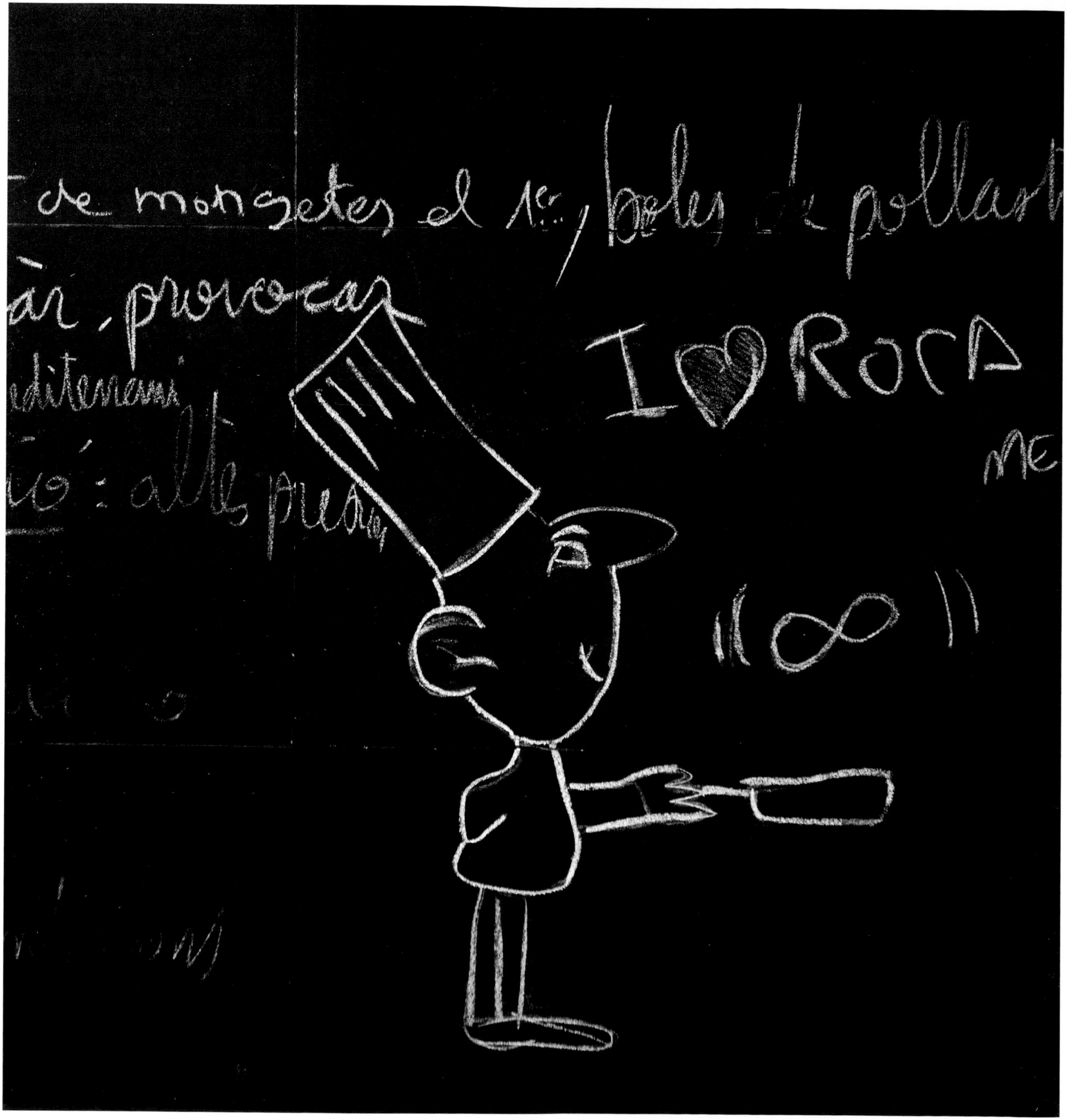
de mongetes
provocar
I ♥ ROCA

Universe of the Rocas: more than words

Let's play a game. Imagine that while you read this introduction, Jordi and his brothers, Joan and Josep (the three artisans of El Celler de Can Roca [The Winery of Can Roca]), responsible for the desserts, the savory cuisine, and the restaurant room, respectively), are preparing their presentation for a gastronomic conference. Once on stage, they organize the materials, prepare their products, and check that everything is ready, each one attending to his own work; they silently glance at each other, to make sure everything is going as planned, and occasionally look up at the crowd that awaits in the seats. They observe the crowd with expressions of calm and surprise, which is typical of the three, as if it were the first time these giants of gastronomy had faced such a multitude. At the end of the introduction, they start speaking calmly and exquisitely: they introduce themselves, thank the organizers, honor the memory of a lost colleague, and start their speech.

Recently I was fortunate enough to attend a very similar event, but in real life, where the well-designed and well-delivered introduction was given by another speaker. Leaving aside the spectacular core of the conference, the earlier moments that work behind the scenes— looked like a magical ballet, rehearsed a thousand times yet delightfully improvised. The speaker offered a perfect summary of what really happens in El Celler de Can Roca: the silence, reflection, and the work, all of which give rise to the Roca miracle; a place where congratulations, awards, and medals are accepted with quiet gratitude. The press reports and photographs in international media, and the unanimous applause of professionals, experts, and enthusiasts from around the world are appreciated and received with grace. To sum it up, talent and humility.

This book is the result of the brilliant career of Jordi Roca, a creator of desserts. As for me, it represents the result of an intense professional relationship that began with his recipes, and my photographs, for the *Descobrir Cuina* magazine, and has continued in other media such as Delicooks, as well as collaboration with the El Celler de Can Roca website. You could say that during this time, the way we worked was refined, like clockwork, and that over time we reached a level of complete communication and understanding. In truth, it was naturally like that from the very first day. Although working with Jordi means photographing the creations of one of the best dessert chefs in the world, there has never been any stress or disagreement in the process. At first, I thought it was due to courtesy on his part, a hesitation to question my work, or a way to facilitate this process. Over time, I realized that our work sessions in his kitchen were much like what I witnessed at the conference or the daily work done with his brothers and partners: perfect harmony and total respect for each other's work, where words are not necessary. I often had the feeling of being part of El Celler de Can Roca for a few hours.

Indeed, in Jordi's universe, things are beyond words. Only a look or a gesture is necessary to see the work carried out. This is the meaning of the book you are holding now: to get rid of superfluous speech and let the work speak for itself. I hope you enjoy it and will be inspired by it as much as I was.

Becky Lawton

Breaking Molds

In the Spanish dictionary, "postrero" (dessert chef) is defined as coming last, but I have taken the liberty of giving it a new meaning. For me, being a "postrero" is vital and it defines how to interpret my profession; indeed, I create desserts ("postres") and not pastries.

My training began in an amateur, nonacademic way in the world of sweets. It was under the guidance of Damian Allshop, a talented Welsh pastry chef who arrived in our home after a long journey through the major European restaurants. He worked, in the late 90's, in the dessert section at El Celler de Can Roca. With him I came to understand the essence of dessert cuisine, its importance and singularity. He helped pique my curiosity by having me as an assistant first and then as his successor. Over time, he gave me the necessary tools to learn the "why" of dessert cuisine, as well as the methods, the importance of accuracy, "to the minute" craftsmanship, patience, steadiness, safety, and obsessive involvement. In the beginning, rules and quantification were basic guidelines. I knew why a soufflé rises, why chocolate is tempered or why gelatin sets, and I learned to actually blow sugar, as if manufacturing artisan glass, and more, and more, and more.

That was the beginning of my chance to create and spread my wings. Since then, I have taken every opportunity to have fun, to dream, to provoke, to amaze myself, and above all, to play. I have been addicted to sweet amusement for over twelve years. I feel an absolute need to express my life in sweets. A walk, a landscape, a smell, a story, a noise, a transgression, an emotion, any road can lead to creativity. Freedom and freshness. Radicalism and extremism. I like to play to the limit, with irreverence and by breaking molds. Fantasy captivates me and I explore my universe in the sweet moment, away from the rigors and seriousness of the main dishes or large plates of a set menu. I like to surprise at the very end, where the boundary between the pre-established and fascination is possible.

In this book I suggest entertainment, a break from your daily life. Recipes that are fun, direct and accessible. Are you ready to play?

Jordi Roca i Fontané

El Celler de Can Roca Restaurant
Can Sunyer, 48. 17007 - Taialà. Gerona
Tel. 972 222 157
www.cellercanroca.com

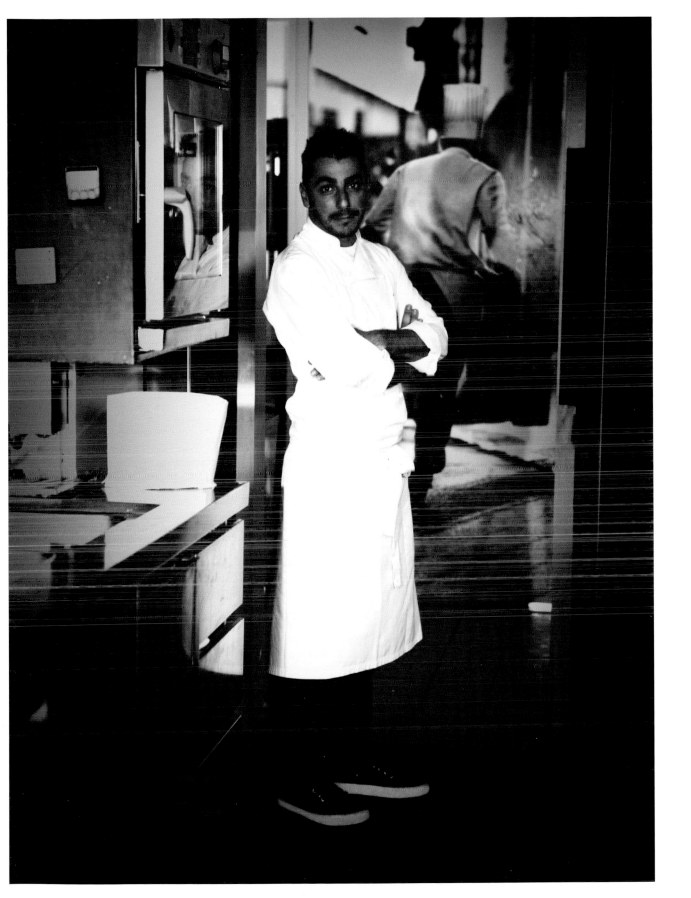

And why not?

Creating an edible perfume, interpreting the taste of a goal by world-famous soccer player Lionel Messi, or a dessert with a cigar and a mojito inspired by Havana are some great sensory approaches Jordi Roca creates in El Celler de Can Roca restaurant. He runs the restaurant outside the city of Gerona with his brothers, Joan and Josep. Influences, sources of inspiration, personal tastes, and landscapes shape a world of aromas, flavors, and textures that never leave the diner indifferent. Roca recognizes that he plays with an advantage when he states, "with desserts, it is easier to steal a smile from the customer." His restaurant is on the lists of the best in the world, with three Michelin stars and most importantly, the daily recognition of clients who come from all corners of the world, ready to enjoy one of the most interesting and influential culinary offerings in the current landscape of national and international cuisine.

This book collects a portion of the work, the inspiration, the discernment, the generosity, and the boldness one can enjoy in El Celler de Can Roca. Jordi Roca accompanies the reader through a playful and imaginative gastronomic experience, demonstrating how to emulate his original and astonishing desserts at home. Included are more than 80 delicious, subtle, and evocative recipes, explained step-by-step with all the tricks, tips, and secrets of the great chef.

The recipes are presented seasonally (from spring to winter), starting with a refreshing pineapple, mango, and passion fruit soup, to a carpaccio of caramelized figs and anise, to some curry cupcakes or an orange blossom bonbon. Signature desserts are featured, in which countless techniques, concepts, and ingredients are combined with the common denominator of boundless creativity.

The open spirit, daring, and nonconforming essence of the Rocas are clearly shown in Jordi's culinary delights. His suggestive adaptations of known perfumes like Eternity, Terre d'Hermès, or Trêsor, his stimulating chromatic desserts or delightful nods to childhood, and the reintroduction of desserts like marshmallows or candy apples make them a breath of fresh air in today's dining scene.

Imagination, freedom, and boldness are the best ingredients when preparing a dessert. A seemingly crazy or strange idea can lead to a brilliant result. As Jordi Roca says himself, "the secret is to ask yourself: And why not?"

Goal by Messi, a sweet tribute to great soccer.

Ready to reveal secrets, Roca uncovers for us what a goal by Messi tastes like: pleasure and acidity, freshness and effervescence, explosion and salivation, naturalness and spontaneity. We will have to taste it . . .

Cooperation, Trust, and Generosity

The passion for cooking that resides in the Roca brothers was cemented in Can Roca, a restaurant owned and run by their parents in Taialà, a neighborhood on the outskirts of Girona. It was there where they grew up, amid the bustle of dishes, pots, and customers. The bar was their living room, the place where they played, did their homework, watched television . . . while the kitchen sent forth aromas from the stews prepared by their mother in a generous, simple, and honest manner.

The Beginnings

In the eighties Joan and Josep Roca finished their studies at the Escola d'Hosteleria of Girona. There, they learned a type of cuisine that was less traditional and more academic, very different from what was being served at Can Roca. At that time, the so-called *nouvelle cuisine* was booming and they organized a trip to visit some restaurants that were leaders in this concept, such as the famous Pic de Valence, halfway between Lyon and Avignon (France). Both were greatly enamored of the culinary prowess of Jacques Pic and they immediately had the idea of creating their own restaurant.

Once back in Girona, they worked with enthusiasm to make their first project a reality. Thus, in August, 1986, Joan (only 22 years old) and Josep (only 20) opened the first Celler de Can Roca. In an exercise of prudence and pragmatism, they took the property annexed to the family restaurant and went to work. There they started serving traditional Catalan cuisine and throughout the years they remained open to more creative and less conventional styles. It was the period when Ferran Adrià and Santi Santamaria undertook new ways of cooking and the Rocas joined this modern and nonconformist trend that sought to break the established culinary dogmas.

Jordi Joins In

Time went by and in 1994 this change in direction had caught the attention of critics. A year later the first Michelin Star arrived in recognition of exemplary culinary efforts, one of the most important moments in the history of the restaurant.

Jordi Roca helped his brothers in the kitchen and in the dining room of the restaurant while he continued his studies at Escola d'Hosteleria of Gerona. In 1999, he finally joined the kitchen brigade of El Celler. That same year, Damian Allshop, a brilliant pastry chef of Welsh origin with ample experience in large restaurants in the United Kingdom and France, came to Can Roca. During his year-long stay at El Celler, he taught the youngest of the Roca brothers all the secrets of the trade, sparking his passion for professional dessert art, and most importantly, allowing him to develop his own personality and culinary taste.

Inspiration, understanding, teamwork, and generosity are some ingredients that never fail in the kitchen of the Roca family.

Behind Jordi Roca's
creations, there
is a process of
bold and creative
experimentation.

From that point on, Jordi Roca began a face-to-face dialogue with his brothers, exchanging ideas and concepts. The three of them have always been involved jointly in the creative process of the dishes. When they face a new challenge, concept, or technique, they work as a team, contributing ideas in different but complementary ways to approach the process. As they themselves proclaim, they dare to be different, but at the same time complement each other in a natural way. Understanding, trust, and generosity are the words that best sum up their project.

A major turning point came in 1996. Encouraged by the recognition of international food critics, they began a second phase of renovation, creating a brighter space and expanding the kitchen. In 1998, Jordi Roca took charge of the pastry section of the Celler and together they began a bold evolution of its cuisine, incorporating various cutting-edge techniques such as distillates, smoking, vacuum cooking, tempered sugar . . . but always keeping the nuances of traditional cuisine.

For Dessert: Perfume

In 2002, El Celler de Can Roca received its second Michelin Star. It was the year that Jordi Roca began working on the deconstruction of perfumes to transform them into amazing desserts. This original and groundbreaking concept was born with the arrival of a fresh box of bergamot from Italy to the restaurant. The pungent smell of this citrus fruit caught the attention of the Rocas. The infallible olfactory memory of Josep provided the key: the bergamot smelled like the perfume Eternity from Calvin Klein. They began to investigate other known components of the famous fragrance, and distinguished natural ingredients like mandarin, vanilla, basil, and orange blossom, among others. They immediately contacted several perfumers and with their professional guidance they began to develop the first adaptations: Eternity, by Calvin Klein (2002) and Angel, by Thierry Mugler (2003).

Chromatisms

Moving from aroma to color . . . In 2004, Jordi Roca launched a new line of work and culinary research based on the chromatism of ingredients. His idea was to convey the concept that colors could transmit very marked flavors and sensations such as euphoria, freshness, energy, and vitality . . . It started with orange, then green, then red . . . The monochromatic plate approach did not quite work with white until they began experimenting with another of the most recognized (and identifiable) techniques of the Roca brothers: the distillates. Jordi was quick to apply this to his desserts, obtaining amazing outcomes like white coffee or white cocoa.

After the awarding of the second Michelin Star, the media attention and critics were increasing and the restaurant facilities became too small.

The New Celler

So this is how we arrive at the evening of November 15, 2007, when the new Celler de Can Roca opened its doors to its first guests. Just over 300 feet from the old restaurant, this space, larger, more luminous and open, planned and designed by the Tarruella & López + Trenchs studio, showed the Roca brothers' new professional stage in all its splendor.

For two decades a team of 20 people had managed to work in the tiny kitchen of the old Celler. Being adjacent to the family business, the kitchen used to end up invading Can Roca, washing glasses behind their bar . . . while their mother prepared a set menu for 200 people surrounded by cooks everywhere.

But those same cooks who in the morning prepared the last meal in the first Celler's 150-square-foot kitchen enjoyed the afternoon in the nearly 985 square feet available in the new restaurant. The dining room went from 263 to 920 square feet, and the cellar from 40 to over 657 square feet. It was a considerably larger space, but destined to hold the same number of tables and guests that had occupied the old Celler: 12 tables for 45 guests.

Located in the old Can Sunyer tower (built in 1911), in the district of Gerona Taialà, the most characteristic space in El Celler de Can Roca is its triangular dining room. In a clear reference to the tandem formed by the three brothers, this cutting-edge cloister is structured around a large atrium area that allows natural light to shine through and has a small garden of birch trees within. All architectural spaces of El Celler are visually connected and open to the immediate surroundings of three gardens that provide a natural and intimate air to the entire place.

The restaurant's wine cellar rests in the interior of a building formed by five large sections covered in wood from old recovered wine boxes. Considered one of the most modern in Europe, it contains more than 40,000 bottles and 1,600 wine offerings from around the world. The interior is divided into five areas dedicated to different wine regions: Champagne, Riesling, Bourgogne, Priorat, and Jerez. In each small "shrine," two plasma screens show words and images evocative of the region while playing different musical pieces linked to the wines stored there. In contrast to other cellars, the wines here are not organized by country, but by latitudes, varieties, and cultural environments.

The kitchen, the cellar, the room, the garden . . . Everything in El Celler de Can Roca breathes an air of subtle elegance and modernity.

SWEET ACKNOWLEDGMENTS

2003
Awards for **Best Pastry Chef of the Year** and **Best Dessert of the Year**, awarded by the guide *Lo Mejor de la Gastronomía*.

2004
Award for **Best Pastry Chef of the Counties of Gerona**, awarded by Tecnotast.

2006
Awards for **Best Desserts Menu** and **Best Dessert of the Year**, awarded by the guide *Gourmetour*.

2009
Award for **Best Dessert of the Year**, awarded by the guide *Lo Mejor de la Gastronomía*.

2010
Paco Torreblanca **Award for Best Pastry Chef of the Year**, awarded by the Royal Spanish Academy of Gastronomy.

Looking to the Future

In 2009 El Celler de Can Roca received the third Michelin Star, the highest distinction of the 2010 Michelin Guide for Spain and Portugal. Thus, the Roca brothers' restaurant became the seventh Spanish restaurant with this prestigious award. The other six are, in order of award: Arzak (San Sebastián, Gipuzkoa), Can Fabes (Sant Celoni, Barcelona), El Bulli (Roses, Gerona), Martin Berasategui (Lasarte, Guipúzcoa), Sant Pau (Sant Pol de Mar, Barcelona), and Akelarre (San Sebastián, Gipuzkoa).

The current trend of the El Celler team is to continue advancing in different culinary techniques, as well as in the research and development of new ideas and concepts—all this combined with the challenge of continuing to find authentic products and raw materials, establishing direct links and relationships with small producers. Along these lines, seeking the best raw material, they have acquired land in front of the restaurant where they cultivate different ingredients.

COOKING AND SAVORING EMOTIONS

The concept of El Celler de Can Roca is established and structured on the work and the culinary research of the brothers Joan, Josep, and Jordi Roca. Their main effort is focused on activating a delicate flow of emotions and sensations through the senses of taste and smell of their guests.

This emotional cuisine is the result of a meditated process of research and development, working with different flavors, aromas, temperatures, and textures, with the main objective of transmitting feelings and creating specific states of mind. Their culinary creations are conceptualized and developed with sense and sensibility. They are dishes with their own soul that make an impact and fill sensitive spaces in the deepest part of the guest: citrus provokes joy, melancholy arises with the aromas of earth, euphoria is caused with soothing ingredients like eucalyptus, and tenderness is evoked with the use of dairy products.

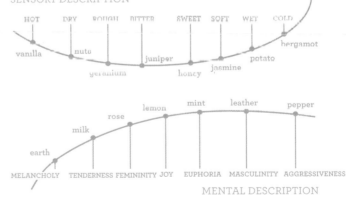

25

A Bit of History

The custom of eating desserts goes back thousands of years. On the walls of the temples and tombs of ancient Egypt, examples appear of the use of fruits and sweets to make simple desserts. Flour, milk, dates, grapes, honey, and raisins were the ingredients used most frequently, although they were reserved for the elite due to their scarcity and were not available to everyone. One of these very ancient vestiges appears on the walls of the tomb of the vizier Rekhmire, under the reign of Amenhotep II (1427 BC–1401 BC). A scene can be found there showing how to prepare a curious conically shaped cake.

The First Pastry Recipe

Vestiges of the ancient art of pastry-making also appear in classical Greek literature. Outstanding works of authors such as Plato, Plutarch, and Xenophon tell, with all kinds of detail, the contents of the banquets where delicious desserts were served. The Greeks learned from the Egyptians how to bake bread and were the first to develop the current concept of pastry, with honey and nuts as primary ingredients. Many of their recipes are known today thanks to the Greek gourmet Chrysippus of Tyana, whose *Artokopikos* treatise includes what is historically considered the first pastry recipe: the Plakon, made with rye flour, cheese, and honey.

The *Pastillariorum*

The taste for pastry making also came to Rome, where toward the fourth century the so-called *pastillariorum* appeared: bakers specializing in making pastries who eventually formed their own guild of professionals. In fact, it is believed that this is the origin of the popular Roscón de Reyes (King's Cake) dating back to that time, when it was a tradition to prepare a circular bun with figs, dates, and honey during the so-called Saturnalia celebrations, and then distribute it to slaves and commoners. The famous *cenae* (Roman banquets) culminated with the so-called *secunda mensa* or dessert, where all kinds of fresh fruit, sweets, and nuts were served. Some of the recipes for these desserts have come down to us through the works of authors such as Pliny, Apicius, and Cato the Elder, or Gaius Petronius. Standing out among the different varieties of pastries was the *artologanus*, of Greek origin, made from flour, wine, milk, oil, and pepper, and setital, a kind of cake made from oatmeal, cheese, and honey.

Sugar and Cocoa

With the incursion of the Barbarian peoples, the art of pastry was somewhat forgotten and it was not until the Middle Ages that it reemerged with the popularization of sugar in lieu of honey. This era in France saw the origin of the guild in charge of making wafers (*oublies*) for the celebration of the Eucharist in the country's churches. Little by little these *oublieurs* expanded their business, manufacturing of all types of sweets and pastries based on each liturgical celebration.

Another historical moment that allowed for the development of pastry-making was the Crusades. During the course of these campaigns, some previously unknown ingredients were incorporated into Western cuisine, like sugar. One of the first written references in Europe to this new ingredient appears in the work *Llibre de totes maneres de confits*, a medieval recipe book of desserts written in the fifteenth century by an unknown author.

The Persians had introduced the cultivation of sugarcane after their military incursions in India (510 BC). Later, Alexander the Great (327 BC) brought the first news of this sweet plant to Europe. Then, there were the aforementioned Crusades and the explorer Marco Polo. The taste for the sweet ingredient was spreading through the Mediterranean, although slowly because it was expensive and difficult to obtain. In fact, for centuries, sugar was considered a luxury item, affordable only for the wealthy classes.

In an ordinance of King Jean II of France, dated 1351, the existence of pastries like cakes, almond fritters, pies, marzipan, and puff pastries is documented. Almost a hundred years later, in 1440, another ordinance for the first time used the title of pastry chef, in this case to grant such professionals exclusivity to prepare meat, fish, and cheese pies, defining the rights and duties of these artisans.

Making desserts dates back hundreds of centuries.

And from sugar . . . we move on to cacao. The cultivation of the cacao tree has over 3,000 years of history. Originally, it grew in Mexico, where the Maya and Aztecs used the fruit to make a bitter and spicy drink, setital. After the arrival of Hernán Cortés to their lands in 1519, cacao was introduced into Europe, where initially the monarch Carlos V jealously monopolized it, making it a state secret.

Carême the Master

In 1556, the first body of patissiers that regulated apprenticeships (for five years) and access to the mastery of this profession was established. In 1592, the Toledan confectioner Miguel de Baeza published *The Four Books of Confectionary Art*, where he explained the preparation of different desserts from that time: jams, dragées, cannelloni, candies, marzipan, nougat, and biscuits.

The craft of pastry was finally established with the arrival of the Renaissance, when the emergence of biological yeast made the pastry industry decidedly different from the craft of the baker.

And so we arrive at the time of the Parisian Marie-Antoine Carême. At the beginning of the nineteenth century, this talented and innovative chef revolutionized the art of pastry, serving czars, princes, and monarchs (Alexander I, George IV . . .). Author of several culinary treatises, his writings provide a valuable guide, analyzing, classifying, and examining all kinds of dishes and foods. His work, *The Royal Pastry Chef,* is considered the first written treatise of modern pastry, with an extensive repertoire of recipes, techniques, tools, and products that allowed an important qualitative leap toward the future professionals in this field.

Throughout the nineteenth century, patisserie enjoyed a boom in Europe and soon there began to appear a good number of pastry shops, as they are presently known.

From the Industrial Revolution to the Molecular Revolution

With the advent of the industrial revolution in the twentieth century, there came a series of discoveries and technical developments that promoted, among other advances, the mastery of cold, heat, fermentation, freezing, and food preservation. This led to new developments in the field of pastry and dessert-making which culminated in the arrival of so-called molecular gastronomy, with techniques such as gelation, esterification, and vacuum cooking.

The trade of pastry-making was definitively enshrined during the Renaissance.

With the Five Senses

Each time we taste a dish, hear a song, or savor the aroma of a flower, we are experiencing sensations. They are direct and immediate responses to a simple and isolated stimulation of our senses. We all receive this information in the same way, through smell, taste, touch, sight, or hearing. The difference lies in how we perceive such data, how our brain interprets these sensations, giving it a unique sense and recognition in our memory. The song we fell in love with, the voice of our partner or children, our childhood landscape . . . these are sensations we perceive with intensity and that hold a very special meaning.

Something similar happens when we enjoy a meal, either at home or in a restaurant. The texture, flavor, aroma, or the preparation of the different ingredients can activate our sensory memory and take us to a moment, a landscape, or a feeling.

Flavors and Aromas

It is not an easy task to surprise diners with a nod to their senses and perceptions. Flavor is somewhat multidimensional and multisensory—it is a collection of sensations captured by taste and smell, the so-called chemical senses (sight, hearing, and touch are physical senses). In fact, 80 percent of what we detect as flavor comes from the sense of smell. Moreover, we have almost 10,000 taste buds responsible for doing the rest, which instantly determine if what we are tasting is sweet, sour, bitter, or salty. In general, the taste buds that sense sweet and savory flavors are located at the tip of the tongue, while the sour taste is captured by the lateral taste buds, and taste buds that sense bitter flavors are located at the back. However,

TECHNO-EMOTIONAL CUISINE

In El Celler de Can Roca deep meditation goes into the conception of each dish. Their culinary research seeks to create states of mind interrelating the psychic description and sensory description of the elements that compose the dish. It's called techno-emotional cuisine, described by journalist and writer Pau Arenós through the following ten commandments:

1 Cuisine is a language through which the cook seeks to express himself. The chef creates for himself, although his desire is to share his work and have his audience appreciate his creation.

2 The chef takes risks: He knows his offering may not be understood. The techno-emotional risks are higher than in other culinary movements.

3 The chef does not create dish by dish. Rather he aims to blaze new trails with the help of techniques and concepts.

4 The dishes are created with the intention to stimulate all the senses. Touch is especially relevant, through working with textures and temperatures.

5 Culinary creations exceed the physical, the senses, and address the emotional and the intellectual. There is an intellectual pleasure which is expressed with humor, with provocation, with reflection.

6 The creator uses the interrelation with other disciplines to achieve the previous points. In this sense new technologies are supported as well.

7 The diner is not a passive being, but an active one. The act of eating requires, for its part, a certain disposition and concentration.

8 All products have the same gastronomic value.

9 Borders disappear between the sweet and savory world, and between the main and complementary ingredients. The ideal form of expression is the tasting menu.

10 Cooking is understood as a way of life. The restaurant is not simply a business.

not all of us have the same tasting capabilities. Certain people are able to perceive aromas, textures, and qualities of foods that for many others go completely unnoticed.

Sensory Memory

Over the years, we lose the ability to smell and taste but we compensate by accumulating sensory memory. As explained by Ann C. Noble, a professor and researcher at the Department of Viticulture and Enology at the University of Davis (California): "From the age of thirty we experience a progressive loss of smell, while at the same time, we increasingly enjoy the smell of our memories."

And so it is that a simple memory can become a starting point for a recipe. That experience can be distilled into an aroma, taste, or texture that transports us back for an instant to that evoked moment. These are the so-called memory landscapes jealously held in our subconscious, to which contemporary cuisine pays a great deal of of attention as a generator of pleasure.

In the kitchen at El Celler de Can Roca the conception of each plate is deeply meditated.

THE SCENERY OF MEMORY

- A walk by the seashore, with sea fennel and waves crashing against the boardwalk that carves through the sea at Cap de Creus.
- The first spring walk through the mountains, feeling how the earth awakens from winter silence and begins to sprout thyme and rosemary.
- The smell of mimosa in February, walking through the botanical garden.
- Wet borders of Salicornia plants at the Aiguamolls (water mills) of the Empordà.
- Mushrooms hiding in heavy cover with smells of cork, pine trees, and ferns.

Extracts from www.cellercanroca.com

Raw Material

Before starting to prepare the desserts in this book, it is important to have an in-depth understanding of the raw material that we will use. Most ingredients found in this recipe book are well-known and easy to find, although it is always interesting to find out more about them. Moreover, in certain dishes we will find elements that we have not used very often (if at all). That does not mean that it is impossible to find them, or that working with them should become a complicated task.

Regardless of our level, it is essential to know the ingredients that we will need to prepare the desserts in this book. Here are the most common ones, take note:

In the pantry ...

Dark Chocolate

Chocolate is one of the ingredients most valued by great dessert chefs. According to Jordi Roca, it is the closest thing to wine in terms of an immense variety of origins, flavors, forms of fermentation, and roasting of the cocoa. To explain this richness and complexity, Roca recalls a trip to the Amazon where he had the opportunity to visit a market where up to 15 different varieties of fresh cacao beans were sold, when generally only three types are known:

> **Cacao Criollo.** Originally from Central America and Mexico, it is a very popular variety for its acid, aromatic flavor without a trace of bitterness. It only accounts for 1 percent of the global production.

> **Cacao Forastero.** Originally from the Amazon, it is the most consumed worldwide and has a very intense flavor and scent.

> **Cacao Trinitario.** A hybrid of the two previous varieties, it produces rich, fatty cacao.

Besides the origin and type of fermentation of cacao, what gives a chocolate its true character is the roasting and chopping of the beans or seeds, which results in cocoa paste, one of the main ingredients for the production of chocolates. Other uses of this paste are the production of cocoa butter (an ingredient in the manufacturing of chocolate) and cocoa powder. In general, the main raw materials of chocolate are cocoa paste, cocoa butter, powdered milk, and sugar. The sum of all ingredients coming from cacao (paste, butter . . .) make up the total percent of cocoa for a topping or a chocolate, which typically ranges between 55 and 90 percent. When the time comes to decide on the type of chocolate (or topping), keep in mind that the lower the percentage of cocoa it contains, the more sugar there will be in the mixture. But the most important thing to check is that the cocoa butter has not been replaced by hydrogenated fats, because then the chocolate loses a lot of the texture, strength, and structure, that are characteristic of an authentic chocolate.

Chocolate candy coating is a product derived from cocoa containing more than 31 percent cocoa butter. It has the same appearance as chocolate but when melted it has a more fluid texture.

Chocolate is a product derived from cocoa containing less than 31 percent cocoa butter. When melted, a more viscous texture appears.

When the time comes to decide on one or another origin, Jordi Roca highly recommends chocolates from Venezuela, Brazil, Costa Rica, or Ecuador, countries that produce excellent cocoa. And once in the kitchen, he invites us to create interesting blends of chocolate with spices or acidic fruits, although the ingredient in itself already provides excellent results, as a central flavor or complement to a dessert.

Sweeteners

Sugar. The main ingredient in the kitchen of a creator of desserts. It is important to master the use of this flavor enhancer obtained from sugarcane or sugar beets. Crystallized or powdered, there are different types of sugar we can use when preparing our desserts:

White or Caster Sugar. It is the most common sugar, white in color, with 97 percent sucrose and fully soluble in water.

Brown Sugar. As the name suggests, it is immediately recognizable by its dark color. There are different types of brown sugar. All of them have an intense flavor and introduce a lot of character into recipes.

Powdered Sugar. It is a mixture of white or refined sugar powder with 0.5 percent rice or corn starch. It is primarily used in decorating desserts.

Muscovado Sugar. It is a type of brown sugar obtained from sugarcane with almost no refining process. Its flavor is very aromatic and slightly bitter (with a hint of licorice, earth . . .).

Invert Sugar. Sugar that is broken down into glucose and fructose by acid or microbial action. In this way, a thick syrup with high sweetening power is obtained (1.25 times sweeter than sugar). Widely used in making ice cream due to its anticrystallization properties, which allow for the production of a softer texture at equally low temperatures. It comes as a thick liquid.

Isomalt Sugar. A product derived from polyols (sugar alcohols), which occurs in powder or granule form. Its elasticity and strong ability to repel moisture make it very useful in the creation of artistic desserts. Many candies are made from this type of sugar and it is an interesting ingredient when preparing a dessert (*see candies used in the Orange Blossom Honey Granita recipe on page 106 or the Chocolate Bar with Candy recipe on page 186*).

Honey. When choosing this tasty natural product, it is important to focus on consistency, because the clearer and smoother it is, the more likely it has been processed industrially. It is an excellent natural sweetener with a high percentage of fructose, a simple sugar found in many fruits.

Based on their plant origin, we can distinguish two broad categories: flower honey (orange blossom, rosemary, thyme, heather, lime, acacia, fruit trees . . .) and honeydew (fir, pine, oak, and other shrubs). The flower honey is more transparent and sweeter, so it is especially recommended for making desserts.

Maple Syrup. This thick, sweet tree sap can be used as a sweetener in making desserts and blends well with yogurt, jams, puddings, mousses, and all kinds of fruits. Another alternative to sugar is syrup of agave, a species of cactus native to tropical America. It has twice the sweetening power of sugar due to its high fructose and glucose content.

Spices

Originating mostly from Asia certain spices contribute aroma and flavor to all kinds of desserts. A pinch of these ingredients can produce very sharp effects on both the nose and the palate. Just do not overindulge in them if you do not want to mask the real flavor of the dish.

Cinnamon. A flavoring spice that belongs to the bay family and comes from the East. In fact, Sri Lanka (formerly Ceylon) is the country that produces the most fragrant cinnamon on the market. It is extracted from the inner bark of the cinnamon tree (*Cinnmomum zeylanicum*); is available in stick, powder, or extract form; and is used in the preparation of all kinds of sweet desserts such as pies, cakes, creams, and biscuits.

Vanilla. This spice is the fruit of an American orchid from whose yellowish flowers grows a pod that is considered one of the most intense flavors in gastronomy. It is available in powder or drops and is often used in the preparation of all kinds of desserts.

Pepper. The intense and spicy flavor of pepper offers interesting contrasts and pairings when it comes to preparing a dessert, especially those containing chocolate.

Ginger. The intense citric taste and the enveloping flavor of ginger also provide interesting contrasts of aroma when blended with the taste of chocolate.

Nutmeg. Introduced into Europe by the Arabs, this spice is from a tree of the *Myristica* genus. Indonesia is the largest producer of nutmeg. With a slightly citric and very aromatic spicy and sweet flavor, it is used to season desserts, especially those made with fruit and chocolate.

Star Anise. This spice of Chinese origin is obtained from the star-shaped fruit of the *Illicium rerum* tree. It has nothing to do with the common anise family but it shares the same active ingredient, anethole, a compound that provides its characteristic aroma and flavor used in the preparation of all kinds of desserts. Jordi Roca recommends blending it with scented fruits like pineapple, a combination with very interesting and exotic results.

Clove. The dry buds (unopened flowers) from the clove tree are one of the most aromatic spices that exist. In the kitchen, they are used whole or ground and always in small quantities because their aroma and flavor are extremely intense.

Cardamom. This spice (*Elettaria cardamomum*) native to India looks like a small pod; inside, it holds dark and very aromatic seeds, with an intense flavor that is citric and somehow sweet. It is commonly incorporated in sweet dishes, cakes, and pastries, but in small quantities because its aroma and taste are very strong.

Fruits

Ingredients in desserts may be undervalued raw materials in other fields, but in dessert cuisine they have great value. This is true in the case of fruits. In several dishes created by Jordi Roca, the concept revolves around one seasonal fruit that is combined with other elements such as chocolate, sugar, flour, etc.

Bergamot. The production of this little citrus fruit with a bitter flavor and aromatic skin is limited to a coastal region of Calabria, Italy. A box of bergamot arrived from Italy at the Roca brothers' restaurant several years ago. They were immediately interested in the possibilities of this fruit, which previously had a long tradition in the perfume industry in the kitchen. As is the case with the other citrus fruits, the skin of bergamot is very aromatic and an excellent ingredient to perfume a dessert. In fact, while preparing a dish made with citrus fruits, it is always advisable to sprinkle the dessert with the zest before serving it. In this way, the aromatic molecules are detached from the citrus right before serving it, causing a cooling sensation in the diner's sense of smell.

Coconut. The fresh pulp of this fruit, belonging to the palm family, is a delicious ingredient in the preparation of cakes and pastries, as well as in refreshing fruit salads. When buying it, it is important to choose those that have plenty of water inside. Once opened, it should be used on the same day or stored in a container filled with water for a maximum of four days. Moreover, the high fat content of coconut milk is ideal in preparing creams, sorbets, and ice cream.

Strawberries. These fruits are low in calories and rich in carbohydrates, fiber, and vitamin C. Due to their sweet taste and fragrance, they are widely used in the preparation of refreshing salads, fruit salads, and summer soups, as well as in cakes and pastries. The strawberry belongs to the group of the so-called red fruits, among which stand out sloe, blackberry, currant, and cranberry, all highly recommended in making desserts and offering some color and a whimsical touch to dishes.

Lime. It has an acidic and refreshing taste, and although it belongs to the same family as the lemon, it is much more delicate, easily loses water, and dries faster. At room temperature, it stays in good condition for about a week. Its juice is commonly used in the preparation of various desserts (it's a good substitute for lemon, and is slightly more acidic) and its flavor blends well with all kinds of tropical fruits (pineapple, mango, papaya . . .) as well as aromatic herbs such as mint or basil. Just like the rest of the citrus fruits, its skin is intensely aromatic and produces an excellent zest when finely grated.

Lemon. In Spain, the most used varieties of this citrus fruit are: Eureka (seedless and abundant in juice), Lisbon (juicy and acidic), Primofiori (very juicy and thin skin), and Verna (the variety most present in Europe). These are the fruits with the lowest calorie content, rich in vitamin C and potassium. Their juice is commonly used in the preparation of cakes, creams, jams, or jellies.

Apple. An excellent source of vitamin C and fiber, it is the perfect ingredient for the preparation of all kinds of desserts such as summer soups, fruit salads, jams, compotes, pies, cakes . . . Jordi Roca especially prefers two varieties:

Granny Smith (green, juicy, refreshing, and crunchy) Recommended as the main ingredient for preparing light, cleansing desserts.

Royal Gala. Ideal for caramelizing and for long cooking.

Mild spices like vanilla or cinnamon blend well with the taste of the apple.

Melon. It belongs to the family of the cucurbits (watermelon, cucumber); it may be orange, green, or yellow in color, depending on the variety. It has an exquisite sweet flavor during ripening and can be checked by gently pressing the base (the side opposite the stem) to see if it is firm or if it yields a little (in this case it is fully ripe). Highly recommended in the preparation of sorbets, ice creams, and mousses.

Orange. The fruit of the orange tree, the most cultivated of all the citrus fruits, comes from the southeastern regions of Asia, especially China and Malaysia. There are endless varieties classified into two major groups: sweet and bitter. The first group is the most widely used in gastronomy, among which stand out the Navel (mostly present in all markets), White (contains abundant juice), and Blood varieties (similar to the white one but with red pigments in its pulp).

It is a fruit with multiple uses and possibilities when preparing desserts, either raw, in reduction, in sorbet, or in a soufflé.

Pear. Originally from Eastern Europe and Western Asia, in Spain the varieties mostly used in the preparation of desserts are the Conference (sweet, fleshy, and with spots on the skin), Limonera (refreshing and with granular flesh), and Blanquilla (green, juicy flesh, and smooth green skin). With this fruit, we can prepare the same desserts mentioned in the apple section, as it has similar characteristics. However, depending on the type of pear used, we must take into account the higher sugar content, for which reason shorter cooking times are recommended.

Pineapple. Belonging to the bromeliad family, it comes from South America, particularly Brazil. Due to its aromatic and flavorful pulp, it is commonly eaten fresh, alone or in salads and fruit salads, and as an ingredient in different desserts, juices, or syrups. It combines well with spices like vanilla or star anise, and allows long cooking with caramel where its juice is slowly emulsified, resulting in a very tasty and aromatic sauce. This aromatic fruit pairs well with liquors like rum.

Banana. Originally from southern Asia, the species reached the Canary Islands around the fifteenth century, and from there it was exported to America where its cultivation spread rapidly thanks to the favorable tropical climate. Sweet, intense, and perfumed in taste, it does not require special conservation conditions, although it is preferable to keep it out of the refrigerator to prevent the skin from blackening. It is ideal for making smoothies, compotes, and fruit salads and as an ingredient in cakes and pastries.

Bananas lend themselves well to delicious mixtures with caramel, chocolate, rum, etc. This said, they are very rich in calories and can seem heavy, depending on the day.

Watermelon. One of the largest fruits, it can reach up to 22 lbs (10 kg) in weight. Native to tropical countries in Africa, there are more than 50 varieties of watermelon with different shapes, weights, and colors. When it comes to selecting a melon, tap the rind and listen for a hollow sound, indicating that it is ripe and juicy inside. It stays in perfect condition for 2 weeks if it is kept at a temperature of 59 °F (15 °C). That said, this fruit is very sensitive to cold and should not be kept at a temperature below 44 °F (7 °C). It is ideal for making ice cream, creams, jellies, sorbets, fruit salads, and summer soups.

Grape. This fruit has a juicy, perfumed, and sweetish pulp, as well as a high sugar content, so its calorie content is considerable. With a similar texture, lychee is also a fruit to take into consideration when making desserts for its delicate sweet flavor and aroma reminiscent of roses.

Nuts

Tasty, nutritious, and a good source of energy, nuts are a basic ingredient in the preparation of many desserts. They are mainly used in confectionery and the preparation of nougat, marzipan, cookies, and all kinds of cakes. Introduced in Europe by the Arab culinary tradition, walnuts, hazelnuts, and almonds are the most common, although pine nuts, pistachios, and cashews cannot be ignored in our kitchen. The presence of nuts in desserts is especially interesting in preparing caramelized and chocolate-based desserts. Furthermore, we can also create vegetable milks out of some raw nuts (unroasted) with water and incorporate them into our desserts. For example, to prepare a delicious pine nut milk, simply mix 3.5 ounces (100 g) of pine nuts in 34 fl. oz. (1 l) of water, blend, store in the fridge overnight and then strain. We can use this milk (or any other made with almonds, pistachios, etc.) to make sauces, soups, ice cream, and sorbets.

Flour

Flour can be prepared from different grains (rye, corn, oats, barley, and rice) although wheat is the most commonly used in cooking.

Depending on the amount of gluten content, flour is classified as:

All-Purpose Flour. Ideal for cooking soft and smooth items, such as cake, because it retains little water. It has a low proportion of gluten protein and works well with baking soda. It is not suitable to make bread because it does not provide enough volume.

Bread Flour. A gluten-rich flour that retains a lot of water, so it is advisable for preparing thick and elastic doughs, as well as breads with volume and satisfying texture.

Depending on the type of grain or its use, the following types of flour can be distinguished:

Wheat Flour. Due to its high gluten content, it is ideal for preparing elastic doughs.

Corn Flour. Obtained from grinding corn grains, it has high starch content. It gives fluffiness in the preparation of pastries and cakes.

Rye Flour. Bread and gluten-poor flour that is not often used for pastry, but instead used for the preparation of rustic breads.

Soybean Flour. This flour provides compact, sweet, and fluffy doughs. It is the flour with the richest protein content and ideal for preparing desserts for those with celiac disease.

Rice Flour. Slightly sweet in taste, its texture gives more density to doughs. It provides a different elasticity than that of doughs prepared with other flours and allows interesting textures such as mochi paste.

Aromatic Herbs

Mint, rosemary, oregano, basil, and lemon verbena are some of the most widely used aromatic herbs for preparing and dressing desserts such as fruit salads, ice creams, and sorbets. They should be acquired as fresh as possible, and as with spices, should not be overused in order to avoid overpowering the other ingredients. Furthermore, aromatic herbs also allow the preparation of perfumed, cold infusions, contributing an immediate and intense note to many desserts.

Egg

The egg is one of the three basic elements in pastry, along with flour and sugar. Apart from being a whole food in itself, its capacity to foam, thicken, emulsify, bind, and color make it an essential ingredient when preparing all kinds of desserts.

Grade A eggs are fresh and suitable for human consumption, presented in stores with clean and intact shells. These eggs are classified according to their size: XL (large eggs, 2.6 oz. [73 g] or more); L (large eggs, 2.0 oz. to 2.6 oz. [63 to 73 g] in weight); M (medium eggs, from 1.9 oz. to 2.0 oz. [53 to 63 g] in weight); and S (small eggs, less than 1.9 oz. [53 g]).

Shell color (white or brown) does not affect egg quality but depends on the breed of the hen or its food. To check the freshness of an egg there is a simple trick: place the egg in a cup of salt water. If it is fresh, it will sink directly to the bottom.

The components of an egg used to prepare desserts are:

Egg Yolk. The yolk is vital in the preparation of creams, mousses, and other desserts due to its capacity to produce cohesion in the dough.

Egg White. It is used in different applications of pastry and confectionery. Due to its emulsifying power, whipped egg white appears in several recipes in this book. It can be made by hand (with a wire whisk) or machine.

Dairy

Milk. It may be whole, reduced fat, or skimmed. The difference is the fat and calorie content. Thus, whole milk has 3.7 percent fat and provides 65 calories per 3.5 oz. (100 g); reduced fat has 1.8 percent fat and provides 50 calories per 3.5 oz. (100 g); finally, skimmed milk has 0.2 percent fat and provides 33 calories per 3.5 oz. (100 g). The latter retains all the nutrients of milk except the fat and cholesterol. The type of milk we use in preparing a dessert also influences its texture and final result, due to its distinct density and its aforementioned fat content. For example, with skimmed milk a much more stable foam is achieved when whipped with a mechanical mixer.

Depending on the type of dessert, we can use liquid, condensed, or powdered milk. It is a basic element in making all kinds of sweet desserts such as pastries, flans, custards, creams, and puddings, among others.

Whipping Cream. This is a by-product from very fat-rich milk (30 percent) which provides almost 450 calories per 3.5 oz. (100 g). It can be whipped, with or without sugar, beating it with a wire whisk. It is used for preparing cakes, mousses, and creams, as well as for decorating countless types of desserts.

Butter. An indispensable source of fat in many culinary applications, especially in baking and processing all types of doughs. However, it is recommended to remove it from the refrigerator about 10 minutes before use (this is what is known as softened butter). Good quality butter should be dense and a slightly yellowish color. It is better to keep it well wrapped in the refrigerator, as it easily turns rancid.

Yogurt. This is a dairy product obtained by bacterial fermentation of milk, normally from a cow. It provides the same nutrients as milk but it is more digestible. In some recipes it is an excellent substitute for milk or cream and it also provides fewer calories (82 if whole yogurt, 57 if skimmed).

Cheese. Depending on the origin of the milk, the type, or the length of maturation, we can get different types of cheese, which serve as excellent ingredients in many of our desserts. As a brief note, Jordi Roca recommends varieties like Recuit or Mató (fresh cheese from Catalonia), Idiazábal (strong flavored, made from sheep's milk), Parmesan, or San Simón da Costa (Galician cheese with a smoky flavor) as wonderful cheeses in making desserts. Delicious tarts can be prepared with Idiazábal cheese and green apple, strawberries with a soft and creamy cheese, or chocolate mousse paired with San Simón da Costa cheese.

Other Ingredients

Citric Acid. Widely used in making desserts, ice cream, candy, drinks, etc., due to its gelling power, among other qualities. It is marketed in different forms (powder or liquid).

Agar Agar. Vegetable gelatin extracted from different marine algae (*Gelidium* and *Gracilaria* species), it is colorless and tasteless with high gelling power. One of its properties is that it can be heated without losing its structure. It can be acquired as strips or powder, usually in bags of 0.07 oz. (2 g) (available in supermarkets). Used in the preparation of all kinds of desserts, such as custards, mousses, creams, jellies, and ice cream.

Dextrose. Also known as glucose, its sweetening power is between 0.5 and 0.8 times higher than sugar.

Ice Cream Stabilizer. It is used to get a more dense and stable texture in the making of ice cream.

Gelatin. This natural food of high nutritional value and neutral taste is widely used in making desserts due to its gelling (frequently used in cold jellies, both sweet and savory) and emulsifying (used to make all types of foams) properties. It comes in sheets (0.07 oz. [2 g] each), which must be hydrated with cold water before use. It can also be found as powdered gelatin.

Xanthan Gum. It is used to modify the texture of a liquid ingredient, providing a denser and more viscous consistency without heating, thus preventing the loss of flavors in the process.

Baking Powder. Emulsifier made from baking soda and other components, which gives fluffiness to dough as it reacts during the baking process in the oven. It is used for making biscuits, cakes, and cookies.

Liquors. The use of drinks such as rum, which brings a marked caramelized character to some desserts made with tropical fruits, Calvados in recipes with apples, and whiskey with vanilla or peach for its aromatic compatibility, is very common in preparing desserts. In general, liquors are also among the ingredients that best complement the flavor of chocolate, especially aged whiskey as well as Calvados or Armagnac.

Pectin. Thanks to its thickening power, it is often used in preparing gelatins and pairs very well with the flavor of fruits.

Salt. This flavor enhancer also has a place in dessert cuisine. It is important to use it sparingly and as a subliminal touch in some recipes. It can be incorporated when preparing cakes and meringues (the salt facilitates the process of setting egg whites).

Preparing desserts requires a certain amount of patience.

A Well-Equipped Kitchen

When it comes to creating desserts, it is important to have everything that is required in terms of both ingredients and the utensils we may need while preparing the recipe.

What Tools Do I Need?

Scale. In this book, most of the measures are presented in ounces or grams, so it is essential to have a small well-calibrated scale in the kitchen. In preparing desserts (especially pastry and confectionery) it is important to accurately follow the measures required in the recipe to ensure a good outcome.

Wire Whisk. Manual or electric, it is another essential tool in the kitchen, ideal for whisking egg whites or yolks until stiff peaks form, whipping cream, emulsifying creams . . . electric mixers can be handheld or with a fixed support (ideal for heavier work).

Pastry Bag Tips. Conical pieces of plastic or stainless steel, which fit into a pastry bag in order to apply decorative effects on pies, cakes, cookies, and more.

Pastry Cutter. They come in different types and sizes, plastic or metal. It is advisable to have a sharp edge to cut the dough and another blunt side for a handle.

Knives. In general, four basic knives are needed: a large or chef's knife measuring between 8-10 inches (20-25 cm), a medium one 6-8 inches (15-20 cm), a serrated one 8-12 inches (20-30 cm), and a small paring knife. The higher the quality the steel, the more durable it will be. Stainless steel ones are most recommended since they can be sharpened more easily with the help of a sharpener, a steel rod used specifically to sharpen knifes quickly and economically.

Bowls. Bowls are very practical for beating all liquid ingredients, or to set them aside as we prepare other steps of the recipe. They can be made of porcelain, plastic, stainless steel, or glass, and we prefer the round type as they are easier to use. The size should be large enough to prevent ingredients from spilling.

Spatulas. Plastic, metal, or silicone, they are very useful for removing the last bits of dough or cream from containers as well as to lift dough more easily and safely.

Juicer. Manual or electric, they extract all the juice from citrus fruits (oranges, lemons, limes, grapefruits).

Ovenware. Great tools when developing all kinds of desserts that require cooking in heat.

Blender. Electric tool equipped with blades, which rotate at different speeds in order to liquefy fruits, mix liquid ingredients, and crush ice.

Pastry Bag. It can be made of canvas (plasticized or not), disposable plastic, or other materials such as polyester. It has a wide end where the mixture is poured in and a narrow end where the individual tips are attached.

Molds. They come in different sizes and shapes (round, square, rectangular, and custom shapes) and in different materials, but the most recommended ones are those made of stainless steel and silicone. It is important to keep them in good condition, since we depend a lot on them for the outcome of our work. Let's do a brief review of the most common:

> **Round Mold**. The most commonly used mold. It is usually about 8 inches (20 cm) wide and about 2 inches (5 cm) high. We especially recommend Pyrex, stainless steel, and black steel molds. It is perfect for making sponge cakes, cakes, and pies.

> **Square Mold**. Like the round molds, the most common ones usually are about 8 inches (20 cm) on each side and 1.5 or 2 inches (4 or 5 cm) high. Very convenient when preparing brownies.

> **Bundt Pan**. They are round in shape with a central cylinder, which allows the dough to cook evenly both through the center and on the sides.

> **Springform Pan**. It has a simple lever mechanism that allows baked cakes to come out of the mold easily. It is round and the most common one has a diameter of 9 inches (23 cm). It is better to opt for a stainless steel model and, if possible, one with nonstick coating.

> **Cupcake Tins**. Stainless steel or silicone, containing several compartments in the form of a small cup for making muffins, cupcakes, or crème caramel.

Baking Paper. Also known as parchment paper, it is a vegetable paper chemically treated to make it waterproof and resistant to high temperatures. Its main advantage is that food does not get stuck to the surface. Therefore, it is very useful in the preparation of baked goods, like cookies, cupcakes, and pizzas. It is sold in sheets of different sizes and its use is very simple (it is a matter of simply placing it on the baking sheet).

Brushes. Available in different thicknesses, they are very practical when it comes to greasing cake pans or baking sheets, as well as frosting the surfaces of cake pans and cookie sheets, in addition to coating the surfaces of cakes, cookies, etc. It is important to clean them well after use (with soap and water) to avoid transference of flavors and aromas to other dishes.

Baking Sheets. Metal trays that allow for even distribution of heat. They are ideal for baking cookies, small cakes, and cupcakes. If they have a nonstick coating they are easier to clean.

Grater. A simple tool that can be purchased in the form of a box (it has up to six different cutting surfaces) or with a handle.

Scraper. Simple yet very practical element, useful for easily removing dough that is stuck to the work surface, to cut it into portions, or to move dough to another container without affecting its form or consistency. It is usually metal or plastic, with a sharp edge and a small wooden or plastic handle.

Cooling Racks. Very practical for stacking freshly baked cookies, cakes, cupcakes etc . . . so they cool quickly in order to be decorated.

Rolling Pin. It is best to choose a wooden, smooth rolling pin, without knots and with a handle at each end. It is important to keep it in good condition, and avoiding scratching the surface excessively during cleaning. To keep its shape over time, it must not be immersed in water but cleaned simply with a damp cloth and thoroughly dried. There are pins of different sizes, but the heavier they are, the better the result of the rolling will be.

Rotaval. Electrical device to obtain distilled liquids from solids such as cocoa, coffee, and alcohol products. The resulting product is a reduction which, if the apparatus has been used at low pressure, will practically not have been cooked.

Whipping Siphon. Cream whipper made of stainless steel, which injects air by means of compressed air cartridges. Usually available in two sizes (17 fl.oz., 34 fl.oz.) (½ l, 1 l). It is very easy to use: simply fill the container with the necessary liquid ingredients, screw the head on tightly, load the air capsules, shake, and apply as desired. With this siphon we can prepare all types of foams (sweet and savory) without the need of adding dairy or egg-based ingredients.

Silpat. A flexible, nonstick, and heat resistant sheet manufactured from silicone. It is placed on an oven tray, and prevents dough from sticking. It is especially useful in more delicate preparations that may break when handled after baking.

Surface. In recipes for cakes and confectionery it is necessary to have a good, smooth, firm surface to work the dough with comfort.

Sifter. It is used to sift flour, either alone or mixed with other dry ingredients such as yeast or baking powder. It is also used for dusting cakes, cupcakes, or cookies with sugar or cocoa powder. As an alternative to the sifter (plastic or metal) we can use a simple large colander.

Candy Thermometer. A highly recommended tool to closely control the temperature of the ingredients we are cooking. There are several types depending on the technology used and some incorporate a laser device for measuring temperature from a distance.

Measuring Cup. It is advisable that it be transparent (plastic or glass) to more precisely gauge measurements.

Techniques

The time has come to learn the basic dessert-making techniques. Besides the main ingredients and utensils, it is important to know how to manage the three mediums (dry, liquid, and fat) and the various techniques that allow us to get different results.

Knead. A technique used for working doughs made from flour and other wet ingredients that can be blended into the mix. Normally, it is performed by hand when quantities are small. Otherwise, we can use an electric mixer or blender that has the corresponding kneading attachment.

Aromatize. To give a special touch to our desserts we can provide flavor and aroma from dry ingredients like common sugar scented with vanilla, orange, lemon, etc. To prepare a lemon sugar, for example, just mix freshly grated lemon zest with sugar (about 0.35 oz. [10 g] of grated rind per 3.5 oz. [100 g] of sugar). Mix well and let dry.

Beat. This is one of the simplest and most common techniques in preparing cakes, mousses, and pastries in general. With the help of a wire whisk (manual or electric) we seek to change the state and texture of certain ingredients, going from liquid or semi-liquid to fluffy. When it comes to emulsifying an ingredient, it must possess a certain percentage of fat or egg. This technique is often used to work yolks, egg whites, and cream, or to obtain a fluffier dough in all kinds of cakes, pastries, creams, and mousses.

To beat egg whites until they form stiff peaks, we must use vigorous, circular strokes, from bottom to top without stopping, until the mixture has a fluffy and light consistency. It is important that the egg whites have no trace of yolk. A simple trick to make the whites very stiff is to add a pinch of salt as the mixture is beaten.

Double Boiler. This cooking method provides indirect heat to the ingredients with a mild, uniform, and constant temperature. It consists of placing a container (usually a glass one) with the food to be cooked in a larger pan or pot containing water. While heating, the water transmits the indirect heat to the semi-submerged container, slowly cooking the ingredients.

Desserts like custards and puddings are prepared using this technique (which can be done in the oven or on the stove). It is also used to melt chocolate without running the risk of burning it. To control the cooking time more precisely, it is advisable to place the ingredients in the water when it is already boiling.

Steam Cooking. Steam cooking consists of cooking food by water vapor, without coming into contact with water. To do this, ingredients are placed in a perforated or grid-like container suspended over a pan or pot that contains boiling water. The rising steam from the boiling water will cook the food slowly without diluting its nutrients.

Fruits can be steamed by placing them in the basket or perforated pan and letting them slowly steam as they become tender. The cooking time depends on the hardness and size of the ingredients. Thus, foods remain much more juicy and tasty, and they keep their natural color.

Cryocuisine. The use of liquid nitrogen in the kitchen creates amazing and unusual textures. With this cooking technique at low temperature (-320 °F [-196 °C]) freezing is achieved almost instantly without the presence of ice crystals.

Unmolding. Preparing gelatin is relatively easy, but when the unmolding moment comes and it's time to transfer it to the plate, it can be complicated. There are several tricks to handle this. For example, we can dip the mold in warm water (about halfway) to slightly heat the layer of gelatin that is stuck to the mold. Then simply slide a sharp knife between the gel and the sides of the mold and release the air. Finally, we place a plate over the mold and turn it over quickly to release the gelatin.

When unmolding a cake or pie, it is recommended to grease the mold well (on the sides and the bottom) and sprinkle flour just before filling with the ingredients in order to avoid sticking during baking. If we let it sit for 5 minutes out of the oven, it will also be easier to unmold.

In the market, there are practical tools like a Silpat, baking paper, or all kinds of nonstick molds that can make this operation much easier.

Distillation. By using an apparatus known as Rotaval, you can distill liquids and solids at low temperature and obtain aromas and essences of any product for later use in all types of recipes.

Making Foam. Using a siphon filled with compressed air, we can produce all kinds of foams (cold or hot) to prepare original desserts. This unique technique of molecular gastronomy allows the evolution of the classic mousse but with far more striking results.

Thickening. Techniques to provide viscosity to all kinds of liquid ingredients. Among the new thickeners are xanthan gum or locust bean gum. They allow a variety of textures, depending on the amount of product used, and they do not add flavor or aroma to dishes and are transparent. Also, they can be used as foam stabilizers, emulsions, etc.

Frying. One of the quickest ways of cooking consists of dipping the ingredients in a hot oil (preferably olive oil) that can reach 356 °F (180 °C) in temperature. This type of cooking makes food more flavorful but also has a higher calorie content.

Gellifying. In recent years, we have incorporated a variety of kitchen gelling substances that provide texture to a liquid ingredient by forming a gel. Among such substances are gelatin, pectin, and others like agar-agar, alginate, or carrageenates.

Jordi Roca is a tireless researcher of new techniques.

Glazing. This technique consists of coating certain foods with a bright, often sweet substance. This resource is often used in decorating cakes, sponges, and fruit-based desserts. A simple and fast icing is made by mixing sugar and water, heating it, and applying a glaze over the food before putting it into the oven for a minute or until it is dry and the piece gets a bright shine.

Boiling. This is the easiest and most recommended method for cooking foods like fruits (preparing jellies and jams, for example). Boiling can be done by cooking with reflux (with the pan covered to prevent water from evaporating and keep the food retaining more liquid) or by controlled evaporation (with the pot uncovered for less watery results). The main advantage of boiling is that no fats are used for cooking and the result is lighter and more digestible. The negative side is that boiling can take away flavors in certain foods, something that can be compensated for, in part, by limiting the cooking time.

Baking. This is a direct cooking method by oven heat. Its main advantage is that it preserves the juiciness of food, ensuring maximum flavor and nutritional value.

It is widely used in pastry making, such as in the preparation of crème caramels, sponge cakes, cookies, cupcakes, cakes, and puddings. It is important to maintain temperature control at all times if we want to get good results.

Mixing. This technique allows combining different ingredients with the help of a beater (manual or electric), a spatula, or a simple fork or spoon, depending on the consistency of the elements.

Reducing. This technique is used during cooking, consisting of thickening or concentrating a given liquid, leaving it to evaporate while boiling. By this method, the concentration of flavor is increased along with the volume or body of the dish. Often used for preparing sauces and creams.

Sautéing. This short style of cooking lightly fries ingredients (in oil or butter) at a high heat, moving the pan at all times to prevent drying and to make the food cook evenly. Thus the foods retain more flavors, in addition to texture, color, and nutrients.

It is best to cut the food into small pieces and use a pan large enough to allow the mixing of ingredients (with a reciprocating motion forward and backward) without anything spilling out. Sautéed foods can be served immediately or be part of a first-step preparation.

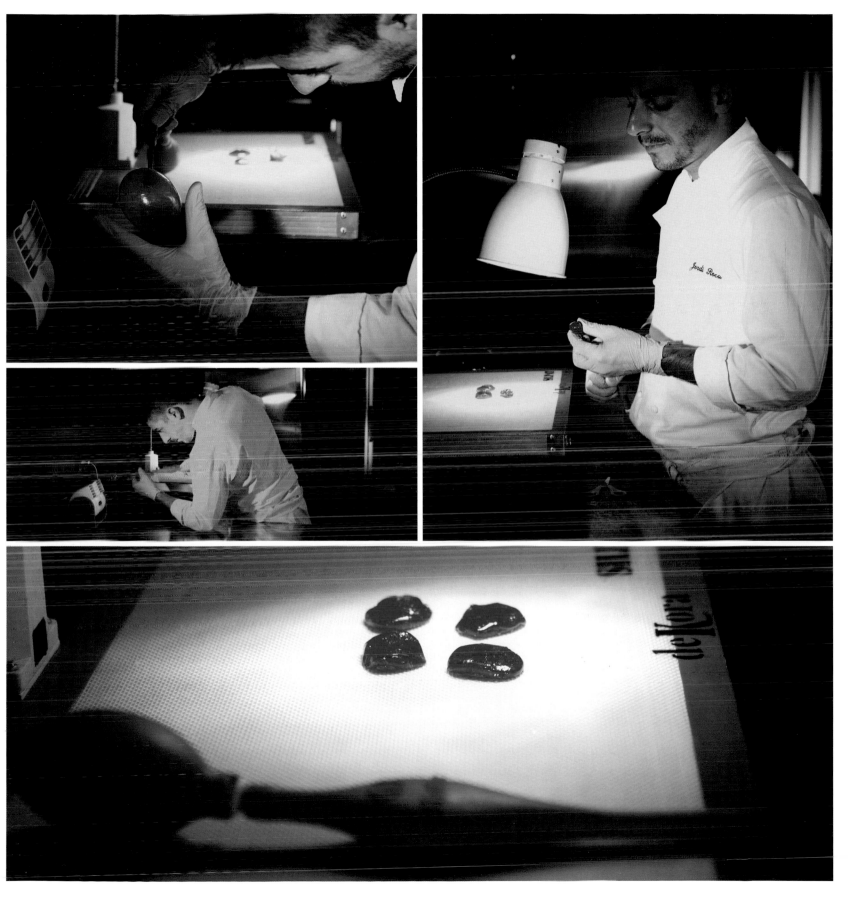

THE RECIPES OF JORDI ROCA

Muscovado sugar is a brown sugar obtained from sugarcane with almost no refining process. It is also known as Barbados sugar or moist sugar. Found in supermarkets, the flavor is very intense and somewhat bitter.

Liquid nitrogen is an element that above -384 °F (-196 °C) becomes a gas and is used in cuisine to make alcohol sorbets, create temperature contrasts, and obtain almost instant freezing.

Ice cream stabilizer is used to obtain a much more dense and stable texture. It can be purchased in specialty stores or artisan ice cream shops.

The **vegetable gelling agent Kappa** is a natural product extracted from a type of red marine algae widely used for centuries in the Irish town of Carragheen (hence the name carrageenans). It comes in powder form and gels very quickly at a low temperature, allowing for the creation of thick layers, or gelled coatings of other products.

VANILLA

6 servings | Difficulty: Very high

For the vanilla ice cream:
17.64 oz. (500 g) whole milk
10.58 oz. (300 g) whipping cream
2.12 oz. (60 g) skimmed powdered milk
3.53 oz. (100 g) muscovado sugar
3.53 oz. (100 g) dextrose
0.09 oz. (2.5 g) ice cream stabilizer
4 egg yolks, pasteurized
0.88 oz. (25 g) vanilla powder
11 Tahitian vanilla beans

For the cake:
26.10 oz. (740 g) sugar
21.16 oz. (600 g) unsalted butter
14.28 oz. (400 g) all-purpose flour
14.28 oz. (400 g) almond flour
0.71 oz. (20 g) baking powder
5 eggs
5 egg yolks
6 Tahitian vanilla beans

For the meringue:
6 egg whites
10.58 oz. (300 g) sugar

For the licorice cream:
35.27 oz. (1 kg) whipping cream
3.53 oz. (100 g) sugar
1.77 oz. (50 g) licorice root
5 gelatin sheets
Liquid nitrogen (optional)

For the caramel gelatin:
7.05 oz. (200 g) sugar
17 fl. oz. (½ l) water
0.28 oz. (8 g) Kappa vegetable gelling agent

1. Start by preparing the vanilla ice cream. To do this, mix the milk, whipping cream, and powdered milk in a saucepan. Heat to a temperature of 158 °F (70 °C) (check with a cooking thermometer).

2. Add muscovado sugar, dextrose, ice cream stabilizer, egg yolks, and vanilla powder. Stirring constantly, raise the temperature to 185 °F (85 °C), and remove from heat. Split the vanilla beans and scrape the seeds into a saucepan. Cover and let sit for 5 minutes.

3. Store the mixture in the refrigerator for 12 hours. After the mixture has cooled, strain and churn the ice cream (*see advice on page 66*). Store in the freezer.

4. Continue with the cake. Remove the butter from the refrigerator and bring to room temperature, or let sit until it is soft.

5. With a hand mixer, blend the sugar with the butter until a smooth texture is achieved.

6. Sift both flours and mix with the baking powder.

7. Add this mixture to the butter and sugar, stirring constantly.

8. Add the eggs and egg yolks.

9. Split the vanilla beans and scrape the seeds into the mixture. Mix thoroughly and set aside.

10. Make the meringue by beating egg whites and gradually adding the sugar. With a spatula, add the meringue into the butter mixture, making sure not to let it reduce in volume.

11. Pour the resulting batter into a 9 x 13-inch (22cm x 28cm) pan and bake at 380 °F (170 °C) for about 30 minutes.

12. Once cooked, unmold, cool, and cut the cake into small cubes of about 1 inch (2 cm). Set aside.

13. To prepare the licorice cream, boil the whipping cream with the sugar. Remove from heat and add the licorice. Let sit for 10 minutes to infuse. Then strain, and without letting it cool, add the hydrated gelatin. (*See information about gelatin on page 51.*)

For the candied olives:
7.05 oz. (200 g) black olives
2.50 oz. (70 g) water
1.05 oz. (30 g) sugar

For the black olive oil:
3.53 oz. (100 g) sunflower oil
0.71 oz. (20 g) dehydrated
  black olives

Other ingredient:
Pinch of cocoa powder

14 If you are using the liquid nitrogen, place it in a container with the correct type of thermal insulation for working with this gas (sold in specialty kitchen stores) or in a container of expanded polystyrene (porexpan). It is important to protect your hands with gloves and prevent the gas from coming into contact with skin. Next, using an eyedropper, carefully add drops of lukewarm cream onto the nitrogen. Remove with a strainer and store in an ice cream bowl in the freezer.
Liquid nitrogen gives texture to the licorice cream, but does not influence the flavor. It doesn't matter if you do not use the liquid nitrogen because the result will be very similar.

15 Now continue with the caramel gelatin. Heat the sugar in a small saucepan and when it begins to smoke, turn off the heat and gradually add the water, and lastly, the gelling agent. Boil again and then remove from heat. Store in a plastic container.

16 When the gelatin has set, cut it into tiny cubes and store.

17 For the candied olives, cut them in quarters, put them into the oven at 140 °F (60 °C) and let them dehydrate overnight. Once dry, set aside 3.53 oz. (100 g) for candying.

18 Mix the water and sugar and heat until a thick syrup is achieved.

19 Add the rest of the dehydrated olives and stir until the mixture comes together, or until it takes on an irregular crystallized texture. Continue stirring until it is slightly caramelized. Remove from heat and store it in an airtight plastic container.

20 To prepare the black olive oil, combine the sunflower oil and black olives in a blender until the mixture is a black and homogeneous liquid.

21 On a rectangular flat plate, place the balls of licorice cream, the caramel gelatin, the candied olives, black olive oil, and a pinch of cocoa powder on one side. On the other side, add the vanilla cake topped with a quenelle of vanilla ice cream. To shape the ice cream quenelle, use two tablespoons to get a sort of elongated dumpling.

Some good advice
To churn homemade ice cream, it must be put in the freezer and stirred every half hour to avoid crystallizing. This operation must be repeated several times until a fine, creamy texture is obtained.

DAIRY DESSERT

6 servings | Difficulty: Very high

For the guava fruit leather:
17.64 oz. (500 g) guava puree (from 35.27 oz. (1 kg) fruit), divided*
3.53 oz. (100 g) sugar

For the dulce de leche:
35.27 oz. (1 kg) sheep's milk
17.64 oz. (½ kg) sugar
A pinch of baking soda

For the foam:
17.64 oz. (½ kg) sheep recuit
17.64 oz. (½ kg) whipping cream

For the ice cream:
33.8 fl. oz. (½ l) whipping cream
17.64 oz. (½ kg) milk
3.53 oz. (100 g) invert sugar
7.05 oz. (200 g) sugar
3.53 oz. (100 g) dextrose
0.18 oz. (5 g) ice cream stabilizer
17.64 oz. (½ kg) sheep recuit

For the cloud:
4.41 oz. (125 g) sugar
1 to 2 oz. (30 to 50 g) powdered milk

Other ingredients:
Sheep's yogurt

1   Start by preparing the guava fruit leather. In a pan, heat 3.53 oz. (100 g) of guava with the sugar. Stir well until the mixture is completely combined. Mix with the rest of the guava, and carefully spread the mixture out on a Silpat and freeze.

2   Continue with the dulce de leche. Heat the sheep's milk with sugar, and let it reduce until it turns caramel-colored.

3   Add the baking soda and let it reduce a little, stirring constantly. Remove from heat and chill.

4   For the foam, mix the "recuit" (gelatinous curds from sheep or goat's milk) with the whipping cream and put it into a whipping siphon, which is specifically designed for making foams.

5   Next prepare the ice cream. In a saucepan, mix the whipping cream, milk, and invert sugar. Boil and add sugar, dextrose, and stabilizer. With a cooking thermometer, maintain a temperature of 185 ° F (85 °C), stirring with a spatula so that the mixture pasteurizes. Then strain, let it cool, and add the recuit. Store in the refrigerator for 12 hours. Finally, put it into the freezer and keep it at -4 °F (-18 °C).

6   To prepare the cloud, put sugar into a cotton candy machine, and once ready, dip it in powdered milk.

7   Place the dulce de leche in the bottom of a bowl. Next place a dollop of sheep's yogurt on top. Then place a scoop of the recuit ice cream on top, cover with foam, embed a sheet of guava fruit leather into the foam and top it off with the cloud of milk.

---

*It is also possible to work directly with frozen mashed pulp and the outcome is even tastier, as it is processed when the fruit is at its optimum ripeness.

Recuit is a very typical type of curd in the northern regions of Catalonia. If handmade, this fresh product is usually wrapped in a small piece of gauze soaked in whey to preserve its tender texture and delicate flavor.

The **cotton candy machine** is a practical and simple appliance that allows you to prepare this delicious treat in an instant.

ZEN GARDEN DESSERT

4 servings | Difficulty: Medium

For the cream:
10.58 oz. (300 g) milk
5 egg yolks
7.05 oz. (200 g) honey
2.65 oz. (75 g) cornstarch
3.53 oz. (100 g) orange
  blossoms
17.64 oz. (½ kg) whipping
  cream
3 gelatin sheets

For the gelatin:
2.65 oz. (75 g) liquid glucose
2.65 oz. (75 g) invert sugar
17.64 oz. (500 g)
  hibiscus infusion
1.76 oz. (50 g) rose water
19.40 oz. (550 g) sugar,
  divided
0.53 oz. (15 g) pectin
2.65 oz. (75 g) citric acid

For the jam:
17 fl. oz. (½ l) water
Jasmine flower
7.05 oz. (200 g) sugar
0.35 oz. (10g) pectin
Juice of 1 lemon

For the ice cream:
4.94 oz. (140 g) dextrose
1.76 oz. (50 g) powdered milk
1.76 oz. (50 g) sugar
0.25 oz. (7 g) ice cream
  stabilizer
21.16 oz. (600 g) milk
7.05 oz. (200 g) whipping
  cream
1.06 oz. (30 g) invert sugar
1.76 oz. (50 g) Japanese
  flower tea (blooming tea)

For the sugar:
7.05 oz. (200 g) isomalt sugar
1.06 oz. (30 g) green tea
  powder

For the salad:
A variety of edible flowers
Strawberries

1   Start by preparing the cream. Bring the milk and whipping cream to a boil in a saucepan; meanwhile, in a bowl whisk the yolks and honey with a wire whisk. Add the cornstarch, continue mixing, and then add the milk and whipping cream, stirring constantly. Add the gelatin sheets (previously saturated in cold water) and the orange blossoms. Strain the mixture through a fine sieve and place in the refrigerator to cool.

2   Continue with the gelatin. In a saucepan dilute the glucose and invert sugar in the hibiscus infusion and rose water. Add 1.76 oz. (50 g) of sugar and the pectin and bring it to a boil. Add the remaining sugar (17.64 oz. [500 g]) and citric acid. Let stand until the temperature rises to 223 °F (106 °C) (using a cooking thermometer). Then spread over a tray and wait for gelatin to set.

3   To prepare the jam, first make an infusion with the water and jasmine. Boil the water in a saucepan. Then remove from heat, add the jasmine flower and let infuse for 6 minutes. Strain the liquid and return it to the saucepan over medium heat. Add the sugar mixed with the pectin and boil. Lastly, add the lemon juice and remove from heat

4   Next prepare the ice cream. In a bowl, mix together the dextrose, powdered milk, sugar, and stabilizer and set aside. In a saucepan heat the milk, whipping cream, and invert sugar. When a temperature of 185 °F (85 °C) is reached, add the powdered milk mixture. Then, add the Japanese flower tea and allow to infuse for 10 minutes. Remove from heat and let cool completely. Then, put it in the refrigerator for 12 hours. When 12 hours have passed, churn the ice cream in a sorbet maker. If you do not have this device, you can put the mixture into a tray or plastic container, stirring occasionally to give it a texture similar to sorbet.

5   To make the green tea sugar, mix all ingredients in a food processer until the texture becomes a powder.

6   Then spread the green tea sugar on a plate and rake it in the style of a Japanese Zen garden. Place the remaining elements (cream, gelatin, jam, ice cream, and salad) in harmony with the occasion and spirit.

Pectin is the part of natural gelatin that is found in fruits and is used for thickening in the preparation of jams, jellies, and desserts in general.

Citric acid is a colorless crystal with a sour taste which is present in most fruits, especially citrus fruits. Pastry chefs use it to control the pH of water and also as a preservative. In this recipe it catalyzes the pectin, causing it to set.

Isomalt sugar is a sugar substitute produced from sugar beets, and contains half the amount of calories.

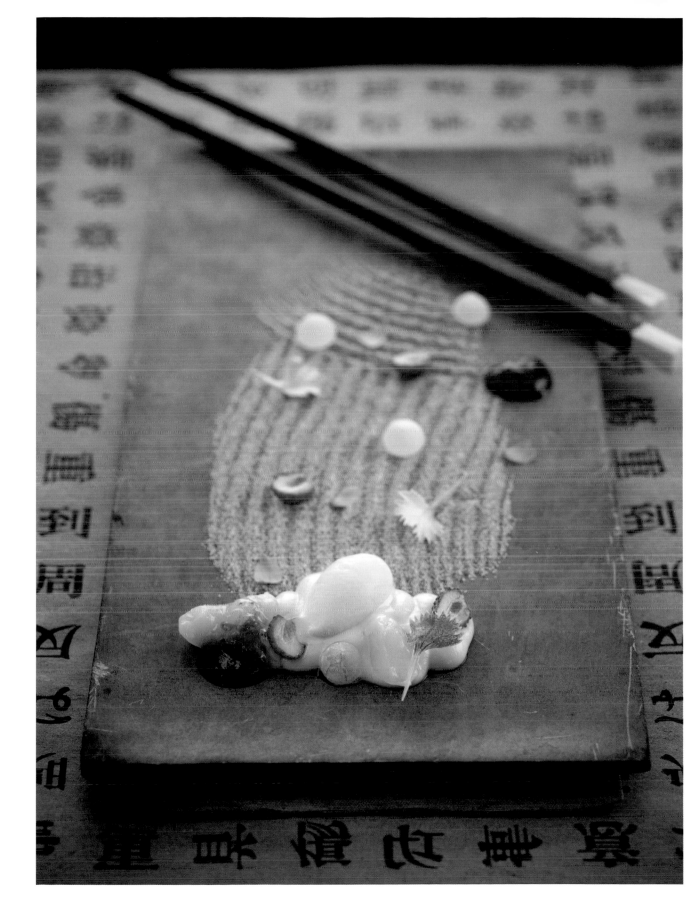

DISTILLED
LEMON PEEL SORBET

8 servings | Difficulty: Very high

For the cream:
7.05 oz. (200 g) lemon juice
2 egg yolks
1 egg
1.76 oz. (50 g) sugar
1 gelatin sheet
3.17 oz. (90 g) unsalted
   butter, cold

For the cake:
1.76 oz. (50 g) milk
0.71 oz. (20 g) lemon
   verbena
5 eggs
4.59 oz. (130 g) honey
8.64 oz. (245 g) all-purpose
   flour, sifted
4.23 oz. (120 g) powdered
   sugar
0.35 oz. (10 g) baking
   powder
7.05 oz. (200 g) unsalted
   butter, melted
Pinch of salt
0.53 oz. (15 g) ground
   lemon verbena powder

For the frosted mint:
1 gelatin sheet
1 egg white
Mint leaves
Sugar

For the lemon water:
33.81 fl. oz. (1 l) water
Peel of 6 lemons

Other ingredients:
Liquid nitrogen
Edible flowers
Sugar candy (see recipe
   on p. 75)

1   Start by preparing the lemon cream. In a saucepan, mix the juice with eggs yolks, egg, and sugar. Heat while stirring constantly until it reaches 185 °F (85 °C) (monitoring the temperature with a cooking thermometer). Remove from heat and add the sheet of gelatin, previously saturated in cold water. Chill the mixture until it reaches 104 °F (40 °C). Then add the cold butter, diced into cubes. Mix it all with an electric mixer and store in the refrigerator.

2   For the cake, first make an infusion with the milk and lemon verbena. Boil the milk in the milk in a saucepan. Then remove from heat, add the lemon verbena, and cover with plastic wrap. Let infuse for 5 minutes. Strain and set aside. Put the eggs and honey into a mixer. Beat at low speed and gradually add the sifted flour, powdered sugar, baking powder, melted butter, salt, verbena-infused milk and verbena powder. Let it stand in the refrigerator for 12 hours.

3   Line a baking sheet with parchment paper and fill it with the batter. Bake at 355 °F (180 °C) for 7 minutes. Freeze and dice finely. Set aside.

4   Continue with the frosted mint. Soak the sheet of gelatin in cold water, heat in the microwave, and add the egg white. Before the mixture cools, dip the mint leaves in the mixture and finish by dipping them in sugar. Let them dry at room temperature for several hours.

5   Lastly, prepare the lemon water. To do this, put water and lemon peel in the bowl of a Rotaval (see page 56). Set the machine to a temperature of 113 °F (45 °C), then distill and store the resulting lemon water. Alternatively, a conventional lemon sorbet can be prepared.

6   In a bowl put a teaspoon of lemon cream and some cubes of the lemon verbena cake on top. Just before serving, prepare a sorbet with lemon water and liquid nitrogen. To do this, use a container with the correct type of thermal insulation for working with liquid nitrogen (sold in specialty kitchen stores) or a container made of expanded polystyrene (EPS). Fill the container with 3.53 oz. (100 g) lemon water and, stirring constantly, slowly add the liquid nitrogen until the water acquires the consistency of a sorbet. Finish the dish by garnishing with the frosted mint leaves, edible flowers, and sugar candy.

AN ADAPTATION OF CAROLINA HERRERA'S PERFUME

6 servings | Difficulty: Very high

For the passion fruit cream:
3.53 oz. (100 g) egg yolks
4.41 oz. (125 g) sugar
17.64 oz. (500 g) passion fruit purée
2 gelatin sheets
7.94 oz. (225 g) unsalted butter

For the gelatin:
8.82 oz. (250 g) water
4.41 oz. (125 g) sugar
0.04 oz. (1 g) agar agar powder
1 vanilla bean
Half of a tonka bean, grated

For the red fruit infusion:
17.64 oz. (500 g) red fruits (sloes, red currants, or raspberries), diced
1.76 oz. (50 g) sugar

For the sugar candy:
7.05 oz. (200 g) fondant
1.76 oz. (50 g) glucose
1.76 oz. (50 g) isomalt sugar

Other ingredients:
Red fruits (sloes, red currants, or raspberries)
Edible flowers

1   For the cream, whisk the egg yolks and sugar in a double boiler over simmering water until the egg yolks whiten and slightly thicken. Remove from heat and set aside. In a saucepan over high heat, bring the passion fruit puree up to a boil. Once boiling, add it to the whitened egg yolks and sugar mixture, and stir constantly over heat. When it reaches 185 °F (85 °C), remove from heat and add the gelatin sheets (previously saturated in cold water and drained). Set aside to let cool. When it cools down to 104 °F (40 °C), then slowly mix in the butter and set aside.

2   For the gelatin, heat the water, sugar, agar agar powder, vanilla seeds (which have been scraped out from the vanilla pod), and the grated tonka bean in a saucepan. Once it comes up to a boil, remove from heat and pour into a flat rimmed tray. Once the gelatin has cooled, break it into pieces and set aside.

3   For the red fruit infusion, add the diced fruit and sugar into the top of a double boiler and cover with plastic wrap. Place over low heat until the fruit comes up to a boil, and then remove from the heat and set aside to cool.

4   For the sugar candy, boil the fondant, glucose, and isomalt sugar in a saucepan to 320 °F (160 °C). Then spread it on a tray lined with a Silpat and allow to cool. Chop the candy, put it into a Thermomix, and blend into a powder. With the help of a strainer, spread it out again on the tray lined with a Silpat. Bake at 355 °F (180 °C) until it is completely transparent (about 2 minutes). Remove from the oven. Before it cools completely, remove from the Silpat and use your hands to form the candy into abstract shapes. Store in an air-tight container.

5   Put some of the passion fruit cream in a bowl and place a few raspberries (or other red fruit) on top. Add some of the gelatin, pour some of the red fruit infusion over it, and garnish with some pieces of sugar candy and edible flowers.

CURD WITH DRIED FRUIT

4 servings | Difficulty: Medium

For the curd:
16.90 fl. oz. (½ l) of milk
6 drops of curdling agent

For the dehydrated fruits:
17.64 oz. (500 g) water
10.58 oz. (300 g) sugar
1 apple
1 pear
1 mango

Other ingredients:
Pieces of fresh fruit
Edible flower petals

1 Start by preparing the curd. Heat the milk in a saucepan to a temperature between 158 and 176 °F (70 and 80 °C). If it exceeds 185 °F (85 °C), the milk will begin to curdle.

2 Add the curdling agent and fill several terrines halfway. Store in the refrigerator for a couple of hours.

3 Continue with the dehydrated fruit. In a pot, boil the water and sugar. Meanwhile, peel and cut the fruit into thin slices with a mandolin slicer. When the syrup reaches its boiling point, add the chopped fruit, turn off the heat, and set aside.

4 Preheat the oven to 250°F (120 °C). Meanwhile, drain the slices of fruit and place them on a baking sheet covered with waxed paper.

5 Bake for 2 to 3 hours, until the fruit acquires a hard and crunchy texture.

6 Finally, put the strips of dehydrated fruit in the curd terrines and intersperse with bits of fresh fruit and flower petals.

VANILLA CREAM WITH STRAWBERRIES

4 servings | Difficulty: Medium

For the cream:
13.23 oz. (375 g) whipping
  cream
4.41 oz. (125 g) milk
1 vanilla bean
1.76 oz. (50 g) sugar
5 egg yolks
1 egg

For the infusion:
35.27 oz. (1 kg) strawberries
3.53 oz. (100 g) sugar

**For the dehydrated
strawberries:**
10 strawberries

Other ingredient:
Sugar (for sprinkling on top)

1　Start by preparing the cream. In a pot, add the whipping cream and milk. Split the vanilla bean open and scrape the seeds into the pot. Then, heat the contents up to a boil. In a separate bowl, combine the egg yolks, egg, and sugar with a wire whisk.

2　In a large bowl, mix the contents of the two containers, continuously stirring. Strain the mixture into several ramekins made of aluminum foil (they are easier to unmold).

3　Bake the ramekins in a water bath at 300 °F (150 °C) for about 45 minutes. Store in the refrigerator.

4　For the infusion, heat a pot of water over high heat. Cut the strawberries in half and place them in a bowl with the sugar. It is important that the bowl is large enough to fit over the top of the pot where the water for the infusion is being heated. When it reaches its boiling point, lower the heat, cover the bowl of strawberries with plastic wrap and fit it over the uncovered pot so that the fruit is steamed for 1 hour. Finally, strain the juice produced by the strawberries while exposed to steam. Set aside.

5　For the dehydrated strawberries, cut the strawberries into slices, place them on a baking tray covered with a Silpat, and bake at 250 °F (120 °C) for 2 hours.

6　In a bowl serve the demolded cream, sprinkle with sugar, and caramelize with a blowtorch. Place the dehydrated strawberries around the edge. Finally, pour the strawberry juice that was stored after steaming around the cream in the bowl.

A good trick
In order to accelerate the cooking process of the cream, it is important to verify that the water is very hot before placing the molds in the double boiler.

PINE NUT MILK TERRINE

4 servings | Difficulty: Medium

For the milk:
33.81 fl. oz. (1 l) water
17.64 oz. (500 g) raw pine
  nuts
3.53 oz. (50 g) sugar

For the terrine:
17.64 oz. (500 g) pine nut
  milk
0.07 oz. (2 g) agar agar

**For the candied pine
nuts:**
2 egg whites
1.76 oz. (50 g) toasted pine
  nuts
Sugar

Other ingredients:
Candied rosemary flowers

1   To make pine nut milk, purée all ingredients in a blender. Store in the refrigerator overnight and strain the next day.

2   For the terrine, mix the cold pine nut milk with the agar agar. Bring to a boil, remove from heat, and fill a mold or baking tray that allows the curd to be cut into rectangles.

3   Then prepare the candied pine nuts. Beat the egg whites with a wire whisk and add the pine nuts, then strain. Coat the pine nuts with sugar and place them on a cookie sheet with waxed paper. Bake at 355 °F (180 °C) for 10 minutes until well toasted.

4   Cut a rectangle of terrine (2.5 inches x 1 inch [6 cm x 3 cm]) and sprinkle with pine nuts and candied rosemary flowers.

A good trick
In order for the pine nuts to be candied correctly, it is important to drain them thoroughly and to remove any excess egg white.

If
you prefer ...
Coloring
or liquor, such as
Ratafía or Campari,
can be added while
cooking, .

CARAMEL LOLLIPOPS

4 servings | Difficulty: High

17.64 oz. (500 g) sugar
3.53 oz. (100 g) water
Juice of ½ lemon
Dried fruit, freeze-dried fruit
  and spices

1   In a bowl, mix the sugar and water. Cook over medium heat and when it begins to boil, add the lemon juice. Continue to heat until the caramel reaches a temperature of 320 °F (160 °C) (monitor with a cooking thermometer).

2   Remove from heat and set aside for a few minutes. Meanwhile, cover the work surface in nonstick paper and lay out several wooden skewers and the ingredients to be skewered (dried fruits, spices) at one end of each skewer.

3   When everything is ready, drizzle the caramel over the end of the skewer where the fruit is to be skewered, giving it the desired shape.

Note: This recipe is very simple but requires special attention to the cooking time. If the cooking time is too short, the caramel will be soft and sticky; and if it is too long, it may be bitter.

MARSHMALLOWS

4 servings | Difficulty: Medium

3.53 oz. (100 g) sugar
0.88 oz. (25 g) water
4 gelatin sheets
1 egg white
0.88 oz. (25 g) fruit juice
Powdered sugar
Cornstarch

1 In a saucepan heat the sugar and water.

2 Add the gelatin sheets, previously soaked in cold water. Without cooling, add the egg white and whip using a wire whisk until the mixture gradually adopts a meringue-like appearance, though somewhat thicker.

3 Add the fruit juice while continuing to beat the mixture.

4 Fill a round-tipped pastry bag with the mixture. Squeeze out small cylinders one by one, (mimicking the classical shape of marshmallows) over a bowl containing equal proportions of powdered sugar and cornstarch, mixed thoroughly. Remove excess covering from each marshmallow.

5 Another way to do this without a pastry bag is to spread the mixture on a baking tray lined with plastic wrap, cover the top with more wrap, press firmly to a height of 1 inch (3 cm) and let rest until it hardens. Then cut it into cube shapes, coat, and serve.

If you prefer . . .
The marshmallows can be covered with shredded coconut instead of cornstarch and powdered sugar. You can also roast them slightly over a flame and then dip them in chocolate sauce.

GUMDROPS

4 servings | Difficulty: Easy

17.64 oz. (500 g) fruit juice
   or water
3.53 oz. (100 g) sugar
0.14 oz. (4 g) agar agar
2 gelatin sheets
Spices, herbs, and
   powdered sugar

1   In a saucepan, heat the juice (or water) and infuse with herbs and selected spices. Meanwhile, hydrate the gelatin in cold water.

2   Mix the sugar and agar agar, and add the boiling water/juice. Add the gelatin and continue stirring.

3   Strain the mixture and fill a tray with approximately ¾ of an inch (2 cm) of the mixture.

4   While it cools, add a few herb leaves or some aromatic spice that will remain suspended in the gelatin.

5   Let the gumdrops set and then cut them into small shapes. Finish by coating with powdered sugar.

If you prefer . . .
You can make gumdrops with plain water and rose water (in equal parts) and rose petals suspended in gelatin.

ORANGE BLOSSOM CREAM

For the cream:
31.75 oz. (900 g) whipping cream
5.29 oz. (150 g) sugar
13 egg yolks
3.53 oz. (100 g) orange blossom water

For the fruit sorbet base:
28.22 oz. (800 g) sugar
5.64 oz. (160 g) atomized glucose
4.94 oz. (140 g) dextrose
0.71 oz. (20 g) sorbet stabilizer
28.22 oz. (800 g) water
2.82 oz. (80 g) invert sugar

For the saffron sorbet:
17.64 oz. (500 g) fruit sorbet base (*see instructions in step 2*)
35.27 oz. (1 kg) orange juice
0.02 oz. (1/2 g) saffron

For the orange reduction:
7.05 oz. (200 g) orange juice
3.53 oz. (100 g) glucose
3.53 oz. (100 g) sugar

For the cardamom caramel:
7.05 oz. (200 g) fondant
3.53 oz. (100 g) glucose
3.53 oz. (100 g) isomalt sugar
0.35 oz. (10 g) cardamom

For the salad:
1 orange
Edible pansy petals

8 servings | Difficulty: Very high

1 Start by preparing the cream. Boil the whipping cream and sugar; mix in the yolks and then the orange blossom water. Pour into cup molds and bake in the oven at 185 °F (85 °C) for 20 minutes.

2 Continue with the fruit sorbet base. Mix the sugar, atomized glucose, dextrose, and sorbet stabilizer in a bowl and set aside. Then mix the water and invert sugar in a pan. Heat at 122 °F (50 °C) (monitoring the temperature with a cooking thermometer) and add the bowl ingredients. Heat the mixture to 185 °F (85 °C) and remove from heat.

3 For the saffron sorbet, use 17.64 oz. (500 g) of the fruit sorbet base (from the previous step). After it has been chilled, add the orange juice and cold infuse with saffron for a minimum of 24 hours. Lastly, churn in a sorbet maker. If you do not have this device, the mixture can be frozen in a pan or plastic container and stirred occasionally to give a similar texture to sorbet.

4 For the orange reduction, boil the juice with glucose and sugar until it concentrates and acquires the desired density.

5 For the cardamom caramel, boil the fondant, glucose, and isomalt sugar to 320 °F (160 °C) and then lower the heat to 284 °F (140 °C) (monitoring the temperature with a candy thermometer) and add the finely chopped cardamom. Then spread it on a tray lined with a Silpat and allow it to cool. Chop the caramel, put it in a Thermomix, and blend into a powder. With the help of a strainer, spread it out again on the tray lined with a Silpat. Finally, bake at 355 °F (180 °C) until it is completely transparent.

6 Unmold the orange blossom cream in the center of the plate and place around it the orange segments, a little orange reduction, and a few pansy petals. Over the cream place a sorbet quenelle and put a sheet of cardamom caramel on top.

CREAM OF LICORICE WITH PEAS

6 servings | Difficulty: Easy

For the cream:
4 licorice stalks
8.82 oz. (250 g) milk
8.82 oz. (250 g) whipping
  cream
3.53 oz. (100 g) egg yolks
3.53 oz. (50 g) sugar
1.41 oz. (40 g) cornstarch

For the peas:
7.05 oz. (200 g) peas
3.53 oz. (50 g) sugar
3.53 oz. (50 g) water

Other ingredients:
Raw peas
Mint leaves
Sprouts

1 Start by preparing the cream. Cut the licorice into thin strips. Boil the milk with the whipping cream and add the licorice. Infuse for 5 minutes, strain, and set aside.

2 In a bowl, mix the egg yolks, sugar, and cornstarch. Add some of the licorice cream mixture that was set aside, and stir continuously.

3 Add the remaining licorice cream mixture and heat while continually stirring until it thickens. Store in the refrigerator.

4 Continue with the peas. In a saucepan, mix all ingredients and heat. Cook until the water reduces and the peas have a shiny appearance.

5 Serve a dollop of licorice cream, adding the stewed peas on top, and decorate with some raw peas, mint leaves, and sprouts.

CUCUMBER SORBET

4 servings | Difficulty: Easy

For the sorbet:
6 cucumbers
3.53 oz. (100 g) sugar
1.76 oz. (50 g) honey
2 gelatin sheets
0.71 oz. (20 g) vodka

For the garnish:
3.53 oz. (100 g) water
3.53 oz. (100 g) sugar

1 Peel the cucumbers, cutting out a lot of pulp, and save the center to prepare the garnish.

2 Liquefy the skin of the cucumbers in a blender and reserve 3.53 oz. (100 g) of the resulting juice. In a saucepan, mix it with sugar and honey. Boil until ingredients are completely dissolved.

3 Without allowing it to cool, add the gelatin (previously soaked in cold water) and the vodka. Strain and add the remaining stored juice.

4 Put the mixture through the sorbet maker. If you do not have this device, the mixture can be frozen in a pan or plastic container and stirred occasionally to give a texture similar to sorbet.

5 For the garnish, cut the leftover pulp of the cucumbers into strips. Set aside.

6 Prepare a syrup with the water and sugar. Mix and boil both ingredients and blanch the strips of cucumber. Set aside.

7 In a bowl serve the sorbet with the scalded cucumber on top.

APPLE AND FENNEL GELATIN

4 servings | Difficulty: Easy

4 apples (Granny Smith)
1 fennel bulb
0.71 oz. (20 g) lemon juice
3.53 oz. (100 g) sugar
3 gelatin sheets

1   Peel and cut the apples and remove the cores. Cut the fennel into small pieces.

2   Liquefy both ingredients with an immersion blender or in a blender and add lemon juice.

3   In a saucepan, boil 3.53 oz. (100 g) of the liquefied mixture with the sugar. When it is completely dissolved, remove from heat and add the gelatin (previously soaked in cold water).

4   Mix well, add the rest of the liquefied mixture and strain.

5   Pour gelatin into various molds or simply on a tray where it can be cut or broken as needed.

6   Remove the gelatin from the mold and serve accompanied by fennel sprouts and cubes of apple.

Of all the variety of apples, **Granny Smiths** are the most acidic and refreshing. They have an intense green color, are native to Australia, and have crisp and juicy flesh.

MINT AND PISTACHIO CREAM
WITH CHOCOLATE MOUSSE

4 servings | Difficulty: Medium

For cream:
4.41 oz. (125 g) whipping cream
4.41 oz. (125 g) milk
1.76 oz. (50 g) sugar
0.71 oz (20 g) fresh mint

For the mousse:
7.05 oz. (200 g) whipping cream
2 egg yolks
0.88 oz. (25 g) sugar
5.29 oz. (150 g) chocolate (64% cacao)

For the cocoa wafer:
1.76 oz. (50 g) milk
1.76 oz. (50 g) sugar
1.76 oz. (50 g) pastry flour
0.36 oz. (10 g) cocoa powder

Other ingredients:
2.47 oz. (70 g) green pistachios (roasted and peeled)

1 Start by preparing the cream. In a saucepan, boil the whipping cream, milk, and sugar. Add the mint leaves and puree in a blender. Strain and store in the refrigerator.

2 For the mousse, heat the whipping cream in a saucepan. Meanwhile, mix the egg yolks and sugar in a bowl. When the cream begins to boil, put the contents of the bowl into the saucepan and cook in a water bath until the pudding adopts a very dense texture.

3 When it reaches a temperature of 180°F (82 °C), add the chocolate and mix well. Store in the refrigerator.

4 For the wafer, mix all the ingredients in a bowl and spread into a thin layer on top of baking paper. Bake for 3 to 4 minutes at 355 °F (180 °C), and separate the wafer from the paper.

5 Finally, serve a dollop of the cream, add pistachios, and a quenelle of mousse on top. Finish the dessert presentation by topping with the cocoa wafer.

PINEAPPLE, MANGO, AND PASSION FRUIT SOUP

4 servings | Difficulty: Easy

For pineapple soup:
1 pineapple

For the gelatin:
4 passion fruits
0.04 oz. (1 g) agar agar
1.76 oz. (50 g) sugar

Other ingredients:
2 mangos
Red currants
1 eucalyptus hard candy
Mint leaves

1   Peel and chop the pineapple. Liquefy in a blender and let stand to allow the foam to separate from the liquid. Strain and store in the refrigerator.

2   For the gelatin, cut the passion fruit in half, scoop out the contents, and strain out the pulp with a colander.

3   Mix the pulp of the passion fruit (7.05 oz. [200 g]) with agar agar, and sugar. Boil and reserve in a straight-sided container that will allow you to make ½ inch (1 cm) cubes once it is set.

4   Peel and cut the mango into thin strips. Set aside.

5   Place the mango strips in a glass, cover it with the pineapple soup and add the diced gelatin, the red currants, and the chopped eucalyptus hard candy. Finish by decorating with mint leaves.

The gelatinous pulp of **passion fruit** has a refreshingly sour taste with a fruity hint of apricot.

FROTHY COCONUT SOUP WITH ALMONDS AND WATERMELON GRANITA

4 servings | Difficulty: Medium

For the soup:
28.22 oz. (800 g) coconut milk
14.11 oz. (400 g) whipping cream
3.53 oz. (50 g) sugar

For the granita:
33.81 fl. oz. (1 l) watermelon juice
7.05 oz. (200 g) sugar

Other ingredients:
Sliced raw almonds
Edible elderberry flowers

1   For the soup, boil the coconut milk with whipping cream and sugar in a saucepan. Leave it to cool.

2   Prepare the granita by heating 10.58 oz. (300 g) of watermelon juice (after blending several pieces of fruit with a blender) with the sugar. When it has dissolved completely, add the remaining juice. Turn off the heat and place it in the freezer until the mixture is completely solidified.

3   Whip the coconut soup with a hand blender or mixer. Serve in a glass or crystal bowl; add the granita on top and sprinkle with almonds. Finally, decorate with elderberry flowers.

If
you prefer . . .
As an extra touch
you can add fresh
watermelon cut into
chunks.

HONEYED LOQUAT ASPIC

4 servings | Difficulty: Easy

4 loquats
17.64 oz. (500 g) honey
33.81 fl. oz. (1 l) water
0.35 oz. (10 g) agar agar
Edible flowers

1 Peel the loquats, cut them in half, and remove the seeds. Leave them in a bowl of water and lemon juice to prevent them from oxidizing.

2 In a saucepan, boil the honey until it begins to smoke. Gradually add the water and agar agar. Allow it to boil, stirring constantly, add the loquats, continue heating for 4 or 5 minutes, and remove from the heat.

3 Prepare four cup molds lined with plastic wrap. Put a loquat in each along with a tablespoon of the juice/cooking water. Using plastic wrap, wrap the fruit pieces into a compressed package.

4 Store in the refrigerator for 1 hour, or until the loquats set.

5 Unwrap and serve the loquats in a dessert dish accompanied by a few flower petals.

Some good advice
For this recipe, we would recommend using thyme honey, with its reddish tint and pleasant taste.

HONEYED GINGERBREAD

4 servings | Difficulty: Easy

7.05 oz. (200 g) flower honey
1.76 oz. (50 g) of cane sugar
  molasses
1.76 oz. (50 g) cane/raw
  sugar
5.29 oz. (150 g) buckwheat
  flour
5.29 oz. (150 g) wheat flour
0.71 oz. (20 g) yeast
2 eggs
4.41 oz. (125 g) milk
1 tsp ground cinnamon
1 tsp ground cilantro
½ tsp ground cloves
½ tsp ground nutmeg
½ tsp ground star anise

1   In a pot, boil the honey, molasses, and sugar. Then remove from heat and let cool.

2   Sift the flours and yeast. Set aside.

3   Gradually add the eggs and milk to the mixture of honey, molasses, and sugar to obtain a thin, liquid dough. Then add the sifted flour and yeast. Lastly, add the spices.

4   Pour the mixture into small rectangular molds wrapped with restaurant grade plastic wrap and bake for 1 hour at 355 °F (180 °C).

This spiced bread will stay fresh for several days due to the strong preservative characteristics of honey.

ORANGE BLOSSOM
HONEY GRANITA

4 servings | Difficulty: Easy

For the granita:
17.64 oz. (500 g) water
3.53 oz. (100 g) of orange
  blossom honey
1 gelatin sheet
0.71 oz. (20 g) orange
  blossom water

For the candy:
Eucalyptus and honey hard
  candies

Other ingredients:
Edible flowers (pansies,
  white ginger lilies,
  marigolds . . .)

1   In a saucepan, boil the water. Then, remove it from heat and add honey, gelatin, and the orange blossom water, stirring constantly. Place it in the freezer.

2   When the mixture has completely frozen, scratch the surface with a fork and place it back into the freezer.

3   Start to prepare the candies by preheating the oven to 355 °F (180 °C). Place 3 to 4 candies in the center of a baking sheet lined with a Silpat. Put it in the oven until they are thoroughly melted. Remove from oven quickly and place another Silpat on top and with a rolling pin, thoroughly flatten and stretch the melted candy layer.

4   Before it cools completely, remove from the Silpat and use your hands to give the candy an abstract shape. Store in a sealed container.

5   In a bowl, serve a spoonful of granita, a piece of the shaped candy, and flower petals.

Orange blossom water is a transparent and very aromatic liquid distilled from the infusion of this flower's petals. You can find it in the home baking section of large supermarkets.

VANILLA CAKE
WITH LOQUAT AND HONEY

4 servings | Difficulty: Medium

For the dough:
1.5 egg yolks
5.64 oz. (160 g) sugar
5.64 oz. (160 g) softened
 unsalted butter
1 vanilla bean
7.94 oz. (225 g) all-purpose
 flour
0.53 oz. (15 g) yeast
6 loquats, peeled and pitted

For the gelatin:
7.05 oz. (200 g) orange
 honey
2 gelatin sheets
3.53 oz. (100 g) water

1   With a wire whisk (manual or electric), beat the yolks with the sugar. Add the butter, scraped vanilla seeds from inside the bean, and the flour and yeast (previously mixed and sifted).

2   Prepare a circular sponge cake mold. If the mold is made of silicone, it will be enough to coat it lightly with butter so the cake will not stick. If it's made of metal, it will need to be buttered with flour spread over the entire surface.

3   Once the mold is ready, pour in the dough and the loquats, saving some for the final decoration of the dish.

4   Bake at 355 °F (180 °C) for 15 minutes and let it cool to room temperature.

5   Next heat the honey in a saucepan and add the gelatin (previously hydrated in cold water), and water. Store in the refrigerator until it sets well.

6   In a dish serve the cake with several tablespoons of gelatin and decorate with the reserved loquats.

IDIAZÁBAL CHEESE CAKE WITH APPLE AND CHARTREUSE

6 people | Difficulty: Medium

For the cake:
12.35 oz. (350 g) whipping cream
12.35 oz. (350 g) Idiazábal cheese
3 egg yolks
2.47 oz. (70 g) cornstarch
1.41 oz. (40 g) powdered milk
5 to 6 egg whites, depending on size
7.41 oz. (210 g) sugar

For the apple:
3.53 oz. (100 g) water
3.53 oz. (100 g) sugar
1.76 oz. (50 g) Chartreuse
1 Granny Smith apple

Other ingredients:
Sliced Idiazábal cheese

1. Start by preparing the cake. In a saucepan, boil the whipping cream; turn off the heat and add the cheese.

2. Beat with an electric mixer until it has a creamy texture. Set aside.

3. In a bowl, mix the yolks, cornstarch, and powdered milk. Stirring constantly, add half of the cheese and cream mixture. Once incorporated add the remaining half.

4. Heat the mixture over low heat and let it boil, stirring constantly. Turn off the heat and let sit.

5. Mix the egg whites with the sugar until it becomes stiff, with a meringue-like texture.

6. Add the warm cheese mixture in two phases, stirring constantly until it becomes completely homogeneous.

7. Cover a baking sheet with parchment paper and add the mixture, to a height of between 1.5 and 2 inches (3 and 4 cm).

8. Bake for 20 minutes at a temperature of 355 °F (180 °C).

9. To make the apple, mix the water, sugar, and Chartreuse liqueur in a saucepan and bring to a boil.

10. Dice the apple into small cubes and place in a bowl.

11. Pour the syrup over the apple cubes and store in the refrigerator.

12. On a dessert plate, place a piece of cheesecake accompanied by a few apple cubes and a thin slice of Idiazábal cheese.

PEAR MILLE-FEUILLE WITH GORGONZOLA CHEESE

4 servings | Difficulty: Medium

For the cream:
3.53 oz. (100 g) Gorgonzola cheese
1.76 oz. (50 g) whipping cream
0.88 oz. (25 g) sugar

For the caramelized pears:
3.53 oz. (100 g) sugar
3.53 oz. (100 g) water
1 pear

Other ingredients:
Puff pastry
Sugar
Gorgonzola
Pear

1   Start by preparing the cream. Mix all ingredients in a saucepan and bring to a boil. Remove from the heat, strain, and let cool. After a few hours, whip the cream to an even consistency.

2   Next, lightly stretch a wide sheet of puff pastry onto a baking tray lined with parchment paper. Cover it with sugar and put another sheet of parchment paper on top. Then place another tray on top as a weight to prevent any increase in volume.

3   Bake for 10 minutes at 375 °F (190 °C).

4   Remove from the oven and cut the sheet into strips 1.5 inches (4 cm) wide and 3.15 inches (8 cm) long.

5   To make the caramelized pears, start by preparing the syrup. Heat the sugar and water in a saucepan.

6   Peel and cut the pear into slices. Place in a bowl.

7   When the syrup begins to boil, pour it over the pear slices. Set aside.

8   On a sheet of puff pastry, serve a tablespoon of warm Gorgonzola cream and add a few pear slices. Cover this layer with another sheet of pastry, plus more Gorgonzola cream and a few pear slices that have been caramelized with a little sugar using a blowtorch.

CHEESE BREAD

6 servings | Difficulty: Easy

3.53 oz. (100 g) milk
3.00 oz. (85 g) sunflower oil
8.82 oz. (250 g) polvilho
(cassava flour)
2.12 oz. (60 g) water
1 egg
3.53 oz. (100 g) grated
Parmesan

1 In a saucepan, mix and boil the milk and sunflower oil.

2 Dissolve the flour into the water and add the mixture to the boiling milk and oil. Stir well until the texture becomes thick.

3 Stirring constantly, add the egg and grated Parmesan.

4 With a spoon, form small balls of dough and put in the oven for 12 minutes at a temperature of 365 °F (185 °C).

Polvilho or cassava flour is available in gourmet shops or shops with Latin American products. It is widely used in Brazil to make the typical *pão de queijo* (cheese bread).

SUMMER

TRIP TO HAVANA (I)
MOJITO

8 servings | Difficulty: Very high

For the cake:
5 to 6 eggs (depending on size)
11.29 oz. (320 g) almond paste
2.12 oz. (60 g) all-purpose flour
0.28 oz. (8 g) baking powder
3.53 oz. (100 g) unsalted butter
3.53 oz. (100 g) aged rum

For the soup:
10.58 oz. (300 g) simple syrup
Peel of two limes
10.58 oz. (300 g) lime juice
3 gelatin sheets

For the granita:
Mint leaves
14.11 oz. (400 g) hot water
3.53 oz. (100 g) ice water
1.76 oz. (50 g) invert sugar
1.76 oz. (50 g) dextrose
2 gelatin sheets

Other ingredients:
Cane syrup

1 Start by preparing the cake. Combine and beat the eggs with the almond paste until well mixed. In a separate bowl, sift together the flour and baking powder, and then add to the egg mixture. Add the butter and mix everything well.

2 Bake at 355 °F (180 °C) for 15 minutes in a heatproof container. Remove from the oven and pour the rum over the cake as evenly as possible so that all of the cake is soaked in the rum. Set aside to cool.

3 Continue with the lime soup. In a sauce pan heat the simple syrup with the lime peel and lime juice until it comes up to a boil. Then remove from heat and add in the previously hydrated gelatin sheets.

4 To prepare the granita, blanch the mint leaves in the hot water for 20 seconds and quickly chill with the ice water to prevent chlorophyll loss. Cool the blanching water as well. Then, drain the leaves well and add them to the blanching water. Chop well with the help of a blender or food processor and strain the resulting water through a fine sieve, pressing the mint well to get the maximum possible amount of water. Set aside.

5 In a blender, mix the cooled peppermint infusion with the invert sugar, dextrose, and previously hydrated gelatin. Then heat in a saucepan at low heat until all the components are well combined.

6 Freeze at 14 °F (-10 °C) (control the temperature using a cooking thermometer), stirring every 30 minutes until the mixture obtains the texture of a granita.

7 Put a tablespoon of lime soup in a cocktail cup or glass bowl. With the help of a round cookie cutter, cut the sponge cake and place it on top of the soup. Add the mint granita and a few drops of cane syrup.

Simple syrup is a one part sugar and one part water mixture. In a saucepan, heat 1 cup sugar and 1 cup water (this will yield about 12 ounces) and bring up to a boil. Simmer until sugar is dissolved. Remove from heat and cool.

Invert sugar is sugar that is broken down into glucose and fructose by acid or microbial action. Typically used in the food industry, especially for making ice cream. You will find this type of sugar in specialized stores for confectionery products. If you prefer, you can substitute the invert sugar for honey.

Cane syrup is a light golden syrup that is made by boiling down juice extracted from raw sugarcane.

TRIP TO HAVANA (II)
CIGAR ICE CREAM

18 servings | Difficulty: Very high

26.46 oz. (750 g) whipping cream
5.29 oz. (150 g) dextrose
4 gelatin sheets
1 habano cigar (Partagás series D nº4)
Parchment paper
17.64 oz. (500 g) dark chocolate candy coating
Candy coal

1   Thoroughly mix the whipping cream with the dextrose and bring to a boil.

2   Soak, drain, and dissolve the gelatin in the still-hot sweetened cream. Leave it to cool.

3   Using a mixer, whip the cream and gelatin mixture.

4   Light the cigar and incorporate smoke into the mixture using a water pump*. This will add only the smoke (no air) and will add a very strong aroma.

5   Once the cream is infused with the cigar smoke, set aside to cool.

6   Cut pieces of parchment paper into 2 x 4-inch (5 x 10 cm) rectangles.

7   Heat the chocolate slightly and spread on the parchment paper using a spatula.

8   When the chocolate begins to cool slightly and is still malleable, form it into small, evenly-sized tubes.

9   Let the topping dry and, with a pastry bag, fill the cylinders with the cigar-aromatized mixture.

10 Freeze and cover one end of each cylinder with the same chocolate topping.

11 Serve the rolls on an ashtray with a little scraped candy coal to simulate the visual effect of the ash. Optional: Consider serving alongside an iced mojito.

---

* We use a water pump, like those used to transfer gasoline from one tank to another. Place the suction on the cigar, and direct the nozzle ejecting smoke toward the bowl, so the aroma permeates the mixture.

Dextrose. Also known as glucose powder, it is a type of sweetener widely used in baking. It can be found in specialty stores for pastry products.

Candy coal. Typical candy with a rocky appearance and close resemblance to actual coal is given away on Three Kings' Day (January 6) to children who have misbehaved.

FIGS WITH HONEY AND RICOTTA

4 servings | Difficulty: Easy

For the honey gelatin:
3.53 oz. (100 g) honey
3.53 oz. (100 g) water
0.04 oz. (1 g) agar agar
    powder

Other ingredients:
4 figs
10.58 oz. (300 g) ricotta

1 Start by preparing the honey gelatin. Mix all the ingredients in a saucepan and boil.

2 Pour the still-hot mixture on a flat surface (a tray, for example) and let cool until it sets completely.

3 Then, peel and slice the figs.

4 Cut a square of plastic wrap and place the widest slice of fig in the center. Cut a slice of ricotta and put it on top of the slice of fig.

5 Repeat alternating layers of fruit and ricotta cheese to complete the original form of the fig.

6 Wrap the entire fig with plastic wrap, press, and store for a while in the refrigerator.

7 Remove the film and cut the fig stuffed with ricotta in half.

8 Finally, put the two halves on a dessert plate, and cover with a sheet of honey gelatin.

CARPACCIO OF CARAMELIZED FIGS AND STAR ANISE

4 servings | Difficulty: Easy

4 figs
Sugar
Ground star anise
Anise liqueur

1 Peel the figs and place them between two sheets of parchment paper. Crush the fruit until you get a thin layer of fig. Store in the freezer.

2 Once frozen, remove the paper sheets and place the solidified layer on a dessert plate. Add a pinch of sugar and burn the surface with the help of a small kitchen torch.

3 Finish the dish by adding star anise and a dash of anise liqueur.

FIG, GRAPE, AND WALNUT SALAD

4 servings | Difficulty: Easy

To make the wine reduction:
7.05 oz. (200 g) sherry wine
3.53 oz. (100 g) sugar

Other ingredients:
Figs (fresh, dried, or
  preserved)
Walnuts
Black grapes

1 Boil the wine and sugar in a small saucepan, allowing the alcohol to reduce and the sugar to concentrate until it gets a texture similar to that of marmalade. Set aside.

2 Cut the figs into quarters and the grapes and nuts in half.

3 Toss with the wine reduction.

NECTARINE JELLY WITH TANGERINE GRANITA

6 servings | Difficulty: Medium

For the jelly:
4 nectarines
17.64 oz. (500 g) water
7.05 oz. (200 g) sugar
½ cinnamon stick
5 gelatin sheets

For the granita:
17.64 oz. (500 g) tangerine
  juice, divided
3.53 oz. (100 g) sugar
Peels of 2 tangerines
2 gelatin sheets
1.76 oz. (50 g) of vodka

1 Peel and cut the nectarines in cubes. Set aside.

2 Prepare a syrup by heating the water and sugar in a saucepan. Remove from heat and, without letting it cool, add the cinnamon, nectarines, and previously hydrated gelatin.

3 Let the fruit syrup stand for 5 minutes and pour it into several individual silicone molds. Let rest in the refrigerator for a minimum of 4 hours until certain that it has set well.

4 For the granita, boil 3.53 oz. (100 g) of juice with the sugar and the tangerine peel in a saucepan.

5 Remove from heat and incorporate the previously soaked gelatin sheets.

6 Add the remaining juice and vodka. Remove the tangerine peels and store in the freezer.

7 Unmold the jelly on a dessert dish. Scrape the granita with the tip of a fork and serve a scoop over the terrine of nectarines.

Note: In this granita, vodka has been used for its antifreeze ability rather than its flavor. This stabilizes the ice and provides a more enjoyable texture. Furthermore, the use of gelatin maintains the granita structure for a longer time.

The best season for **nectarines** is in July. This is the time to enjoy the sweet, refreshing taste of this genetic variant of peach, which is smaller and has a smoother skin.

WARM PEACH CREAM

4 servings | Difficulty: Medium

For cream:
3 peaches
7.05 oz. (200 g) water
3.53 oz. (100 g) sugar
1.76 oz. (50 g) unsalted
   butter

For the cake:
8.82 oz. (250 g) sugar
3.53 oz. (100 g) almond flour
3.53 oz. (100 g) all-purpose
   flour
Pinch of salt
3 egg whites
5.29 oz. (150 g) unsalted
   butter, melted
1 vanilla bean

For the sorbet:
8.82 oz. (250 g) peach pulp,
   divided
3.53 oz. (100 g) sugar
1.76 oz. (50 g) honey
1 gelatin sheet

1 Start by preparing the cream. Peel and chop the peaches.

2 In a pot, boil the water and sugar. Add the pieces of peach and continue cooking until the fruit is very soft.

3 Remove the pan from the heat and puree the mixture in a blender until a very fine texture is achieved.

4 Add the butter, cut into small cubes, and continue stirring. Store in the refrigerator.

5 To prepare the cake, sift and mix the sugar, flours, and salt.

6 In a bowl, gradually mix the egg whites, flour mixture, and butter. Split the vanilla bean, scrape out the seeds, and mix them into the bowl. Store in the refrigerator overnight.

7 The next day, put the mixture into a baking tray previously greased with butter and dusted with flour. Bake in the oven at 390 °F (200 °C) for about 15 minutes. Set aside.

8 Prepare the sorbet. In a saucepan, heat 3.53 oz. (100 g) of peach pulp with the sugar and honey.

9 Remove from heat and, before it cools, add the gelatin (previously hydrated) and the rest of the pulp.

10 Place the mix in the sorbet machine and store in the freezer. If you do not have this device, the mixture can be frozen in a pan or plastic container and stirred occasionally to give a texture similar to sorbet.

11 Serve the warm cream in a cup or bowl along with a piece of sponge cake and a scoop of sorbet on top.

If
you prefer ...
In order to achieve
a lighter and more
aromatic cream
you can lighten it
using olive oil
in place of butter.

BAKED APRICOTS WITH FINE HERBS

4 servings | Difficulty: Easy

For the apricots:
8 apricots
3.53 oz. (100 g) sugar
3.53 oz. (100 g) unsalted
   butter
1.76 oz. (50 g) honey
Aromatic herbs (rosemary,
   thyme, lemon verbena,
   hyssop, bay . . .) to taste

For the granita:
17.64 oz. (500 g) apricot
   pulp, divided
3.53 oz. (100 g) sugar
2 gelatin sheets
1.76 oz. (50 g) apricot liqueur

1 In a casserole or baking pan, mix the apricots with the sugar, butter, honey, and aromatic herbs. Bake at 320 °F (160 °C) for 20 minutes. Set aside.

2 Prepare the granita in a saucepan by heating 3.53 oz. (100 g) apricot pulp and the sugar.

3 Bring to boil, remove from heat, and stir in the gelatin (previously saturated in cold water).

4 Add the remaining pulp and apricot liqueur. Store in the freezer.

5 Serve 2 or 3 apricots (depending on size) on a dessert dish accompanied by the granita.

A good trick
For the apricots to be tender when baked, choose fruit that is fully ripe.

If you prefer....
You can substitute the apricots with plums or other seasonal fruits.

TOMATO AND STRAWBERRY GAZPACHO

4 servings | Difficulty: Easy

8.81 oz. (250 g) tomatoes
8.81 oz. (250 g) strawberries
3.53 oz. (50 g) sugar
0.53 oz. (15 g) extra virgin
  olive oil
Salt and pepper
Aromatic herbs (rosemary,
  thyme, mint, basil ...)
Additional strawberries and
  tomatoes for salad, diced

1 Blend the tomatoes and strawberries with an immersion or standard blender.

2 Add sugar, oil, and salt and pepper to taste. Add a pinch of rosemary and thyme. Mix everything with a hand mixer and strain.

3 In a bowl, prepare a small salad with the diced strawberries and tomatoes. Add a few mint leaves and basil. Pour the sweet gazpacho on top and serve.

A little tip
For the gazpacho to have a well-balanced flavor, it is important to use fully ripe tomatoes and strawberries.

If you prefer ... You can finish off the dish by adding a few flakes of sea salt.

If
you prefer . . .
Muscovado sugar can
be used instead of white
sugar. In this manner a more
intense and engaging
flavor will be achieved.

GUACAMOLE WITH LIME AND PINEAPPLE

4 servings | Difficulty: Easy

In this recipe, we suggest the use of avocado as the creamy and texturizing element. The lime contributes a touch of acidity which contrasts with the aroma of the pineapple and the balsamic hint of the tarragon leaves.

2 avocados
3.53 oz. (100 g) sugar
1 lime (peel and juice)
½ pineapple
Tarragon leaves

1 Peel and mash the avocados.

2 Add the sugar, grated lime peel, and its juice. Mix and mash until you get a very fine emulsion.

3 Cut the pineapple into small cubes.

4 In a bowl or a soup plate, put some guacamole alternating with bits of pineapple and tarragon leaves.

The fresh **tarragon** leaves bring an intense flavor to the dish, with an anise-y, slightly spicy touch.

GREEN CHROMATISM

8 servings | Difficulty: Very high

For the candies:
4.23 oz. (120 g) sugar
1.41 oz. (40 g) water
0.88 oz. (25 g) Green
    Chartreuse
Cornstarch

For the sorbet:
18.17 oz. (515 g) cucumber
    juice
4.23 oz. (120 g) sugar
Pinch of salt
0.18 oz. (5 g) sorbet
    stabilizer

For the granita:
35.27 oz. (1 kg) melon juice,
    divided
3.53 oz. (100 g) dextrose
3.53 oz. (100 g) invert sugar
8 gelatin sheets

For the oil:
3.53 oz. (100 g) liquefied
    cucumber skin
1.76 oz. (50 g) olive oil

Other ingredients:
2 cucumbers
Mint leaves
Mint flowers

1   Start with the candies. Mix and heat the sugar and water at a temperature of 228 °F (109 °C) (controlled with the help of a cooking thermometer). Remove from heat, let cool slightly, and add the Green Chartreuse. Set aside.

2   Fill a plate or tray to about 1.5 inches (4 cm) high with cornstarch and bake at 176 °F (80 °C) for several hours to remove moisture from this ingredient.

3   Remove the tray from the oven, press, smooth it out, and make small holes. Fill the holes with the mixture of syrup and Chartreuse.

4   Lightly sprinkle the surface with additional dry cornstarch and return to oven at 104 °F (40 °C) for 24 hours to ensure that the syrup and the liqueur in the candies crystallize.

5   Remove the candies very carefully and remove the excess cornstarch with a brush. Set aside.

6   Prepare the cucumber sorbet by mixing all ingredients. Heat at a temperature of 185 °F (85 °C). Then, put the mixture in a blender and puree. Move the mixture into the refrigerator and cool for 12 hours. Then add the mixture to an ice cream maker. If you do not have this small appliance, you can put the mixture in the freezer on a tray and stir every two hours so that the crystals formed are very small. Store at -40 °F (-18 °C).

7   Prepare the melon granita. In a saucepan, mix 7.05 oz. (200 g) melon juice, dextrose, and invert sugar. Heat just enough to dissolve the sugars and, before it cools, add the gelatin and the remaining melon juice, and mix well with the other ingredients.

8   To prepare the oil, peel the cucumber, liquefy its skin in a food processor, and bind it with a little bit of olive oil.

9   Cut some thin strips of the unused cucumber. In a bowl, place the slices of cucumber, Chartreuse candies, sorbet, cucumber oil, and a few mint leaves and flowers.

Chartreuse is a traditional herbal liqueur from France. Its name is related to the Arthurian monastery Grande-Chartreuse (near Grenoble) from which it comes. It is made from more than 100 herbs macerated in grape alcohol and distilled afterward.

CARAMELIZED APRICOT

8 servings | Difficulty: Very high

For the foam:

3.53 oz. (100 g) sugar
17.64 oz. (500 g) apricot pulp
  (about 28.22 oz. [800 g])
  whole fruit is needed)
1.76 oz. (50 g) unsalted
  butter
11.46 oz. (325 g) pasteurized
  egg whites

For the cake:

21.16 oz. (600 g) unsalted
  butter
36.68 oz. (1040 g) sugar,
  divided
14.11 oz. (400 g) all-purpose
  flour
14.11 oz. (400 g) almond
  flour
.71 oz. (20 g) baking powder
14.11 oz. (400 g) eggs
5.64 oz. (160 g) egg yolks
6 vanilla beans
14.11 oz. (400 g) egg whites

For the ice cream:

10.58 oz. (300 g) milk
3.53 oz. (100 g) whipping
  cream
0.88 oz. (25 g) invert sugar
1.76 oz. (50 g) sugar
0.88 oz. (25 g) dextrose
0.71 oz. (20 g) milk powder
0.07 oz. (2 g) ice cream
  stabilizer
5 apricot kernels, shelled

For the caramel candies:

8.82 oz. (250 g) fondant
4.41 oz. (125 g) glucose
4.41 oz. (125 g) isomalt sugar
10 drops of citric acid in a
  50% solution

1 Start by preparing the hot apricot foam. In a saucepan, heat the sugar at low heat and then slow down the cooking of the caramel by adding the apricot pulp. Add the butter and boil. Strain, cool, and add the egg whites. Set aside.

2 For the cake, beat the butter and 26.10 oz. (740 g) of the sugar in an electric mixer. In a separate bowl, sift together the flour, almond flour, and baking powder. Then add to the butter and sugar mixture, stirring constantly to fully incorporate. Add the eggs, egg yolks, and vanilla seeds (which have been scraped out from the vanilla beans) and mix. In a separate bowl, beat the egg whites and remaining sugar until you get a stiff meringue consistency. Use a spatula to incorporate the meringue into the other mixture, being careful not to lose the fluffiness. Spread the batter in a pan (about 8 x 12 inches [20 x 30 cm]). Bake at 355 °F (180 °C) for 15 minutes or until done (when a toothpick inserted comes out clean). Cool and set aside.

3 For the ice cream, heat the milk, cream, and invert sugar at 122 °F (50 °C). Meanwhile, mix the sugar, dextrose, milk powder, and stabilizer. Add this group of dry elements to the liquid mixture, raise the temperature to 185 °F (85 °C), turn off the heat, and cool as quickly as possible. Add the apricot kernels, and grind the mixture in a food processor. Let infuse for at least 12 hours in the refrigerator at about 39 °F (4 °C).

4 For the caramel, put all the sugars in a saucepan and heat up to 302 °F (150 °C). Add the citric acid and raise the temperature to 320 °F (160 °C). Remove, let cool a little, and place it on a Silpat. Work the caramel by stretching and kneading it about 20 times. Cut it into small balls of 0.5 inches (1 cm) in diameter and, with the help of an air pump, blow to form small apricots. Finally, cut the end that connects them to the pump and store them in a dry place.

5 Cut the cake into small cubes and place a few on a plate. Place the apricot foam mixture (from step #1) into a whipping siphon and use it to fill a caramel candy ball with the foam. Place the ball on top of the cake, and then place a quenelle of ice cream next to it.

Pasteurized egg white is a liquid prepared and packaged for use in the kitchen. The pasteurization process removes any bacteria and has the advantage of simplifying the work of cracking and separating the whites from the yolks. Egg whites are highly recommended for athletes and people who need an extra dose of protein without any fat.

GRILLED WATERMELON WITH ALMOND AND VODKA GRANITA

4 servings | Difficulty: Medium

For the granita:
21.16 oz. (600 g) watermelon
3.53 oz. (100 g) sugar
2 gelatin sheets
0.88 oz. (25 g) vodka

Other ingredients:
4 strips of watermelon
(0.5 inch (1 cm) high, 1 inch
(2 cm) wide, and 1.5 inches
(4 cm) long)
Raw almonds, sliced

1 Start by preparing the granita. Cut the watermelon into small pieces and liquefy with the help of a blender or immersion blender. Strain.

2 In a saucepan, heat 3.53 oz. (100 g) watermelon juice and sugar. Let boil, remove from heat, and add the gelatin (previously saturated in cold water).

3 Add the remaining watermelon juice and vodka. Store in the freezer.

4 Heat a nonstick paella pan and lightly grill the watermelon strips on both sides.

5 In a bowl, place two strips of grilled watermelon with the granita in the middle and the raw almonds on top.

Remember
It is important that the surface of the paella pan is very hot for the watermelon to caramelize quickly and not to lose very much water.

MELON AND TARRAGON POPSICLES

4 servings | Difficulty: Medium

For the syrup:
14.11 oz. (400 g) water
7.05 oz. (200 g) sugar
1.76 oz. (50 g) melon liqueur

For the gelatin:
33.81 fl. oz. (1 l) water
7.05 oz. (200 g) sugar
3.53 oz. (100 g) tarragon
  leaves
8 gelatin sheets

Other ingredient:
1 melon

1 In a saucepan, heat the water and sugar. Add the liqueur and store in an airtight plastic container.

2 For the gelatin, boil the water and sugar. As soon as it reaches the boiling point, blanch the tarragon leaves for 20 seconds and quickly immerse them in cold water, then remove and set aside. Let the cooking water cool.

3 In a blender, mix the tarragon and cooking water. Puree until the water is a tarragon green-ish color. Strain and then add the gelatin sheets (previously hydrated), and mix until they dissolve. Store in an airtight plastic container.

4 For the popsicle, cut the melon in rectangles and immerse them in the sugar syrup (that you created in step #1) overnight.

5 The next day, insert a wooden stick in one end of each melon rectangle and store in the freezer for a few hours.

6 Once frozen, coat the melon popsicles with the tarragon gelatin several times. This will turn the melon a green color. You may also choose to leave some of the popsicles as they are (without the tarragon gelatin) to provide color variety.

7 Serve the popsicles in a bowl accompanied by fresh tarragon leaves.

CANTALOUPE MELON BROCHETTE

4 servings | Difficulty: Medium

For the meringue:
6 egg whites
3.53 oz. (100 g) sugar
Juice of ½ lemon
1.76 oz. (50 g) grated
  coconut

Other ingredients:
Honeydew melon
Mint, basil, tarragon,
  fennel leaves . . .

1 Beat the egg whites and slowly sprinkle in the sugar and lemon juice. Mix until the consistency is very stiff. Sprinkle the grated coconut in while stirring continuously.

2 Using a melon baller, scoop two or three melon balls per brochette. Stick through the melon balls and coat with coconut meringue.

3 Finally, sprinkle the brochette with coconut and aromatic leaves

A good trick
The meringue can be slightly burned with the help of a kitchen torch to give it a roasted touch.

EGG WHITE WITH BEER FOAM

4 servings | Difficulty: Medium

For the beer foam:
2 gelatin sheets
0.71 oz. (20 g) buckwheat
 beer (Keks)
0.35 oz. (10 g) sugar
0.07 oz. (2 g) baking soda

For the gelatin:
1.76 oz. (50 g) sugar
0.35 ounces (10 g) of lemon
 juice
0.11 oz. (3 g) agar agar

1 Soak the gelatin sheets in cold water until they are hydrated and may be dissolved thoroughly.

2 In a saucepan, heat half of the beer and all of the sugar. When it begins to dissolve, incorporate the gelatin, remaining beer, and baking soda. Stirring constantly, put the mixture into a whipping siphon *(see page 56)*. Store in the refrigerator for at least 2 hours.

3 In a saucepan, mix the sugar, lemon juice, and agar agar. Heat, stirring constantly, and let boil for one minute.

4 Without letting it cool, pour the juice into several cups and let rest at room temperature for 30 minutes. Store in the refrigerator.

5 Add two loads of CO_2 in the foam siphon (according to the manufacturer's instructions), shake, and fill the prepared juice cups with beer foam. Serve very cold.

Buckwheat beer is made using traditional malted barley, hops, and buckwheat flower, a pseudo-grain from Central Asia; it is a very good source of energy, nutritious, and suitable for people with celiac disease.

WHITE SANGRIA

4 servings | Difficulty: Easy

For the sangria granita:
8.82 oz. (250 g) water
3.53 oz. (100 g) sugar
0.71 oz. (20 g) lemon juice
1 cinnamon stick
Zest of 1 lemon
1 teaspoon orange liqueur
   (Cointreau type)
16.91 fl. oz. (½ l) white wine

For brochette:
1 peach
1 melon
3.53 oz. (100 g) strawberries
1 apple

1   In a saucepan, heat the water, sugar, and lemon juice. When it reaches the boiling point, remove from heat and add the cinnamon and lemon zest.

2   Infuse for 5 minutes, strain, and mix with the orange liqueur and wine. Store in a container suitable for the freezer for at least 8 hours.

3   For the brochette, dice the peach, melon, strawberries and apple. Thread them onto wooden skewers. Serve a little bit of shaven sangria in small glasses (previously frozen in the freezer) accompanied by the brochette.

If
you prefer . . .
You can serve the
sangria as a regular liquid
drink by not freezing it.

GIN TONIC

4 servings | Difficulty: Medium

For the cream:
1 gelatin sheet
10.58 oz. (300 g) whipping
   cream
1.76 oz. (50 g) sugar
0.18 oz. (5 g) juniper powder

For the cubes:
2 gelatin sheets
7.05 oz. (200 g) water
3.53 oz. (100 g) sugar
1.76 oz. (50 g) lemon juice
Zest of 2 lemons

For the gelatin:
3 gelatin sheets
1.41 oz. (40 g) water
1.41 oz. (40 g) sugar
14.11 oz. (400 g) tonic water
1.41 oz. (40 g) gin

1 Start by preparing the juniper cream. Soak the gelatin in cold water to hydrate.

2 Meanwhile, in a saucepan, heat the whipping cream, sugar, and juniper powder. When it comes to a boil, add the gelatin, mix, and then remove from heat. Let it rest until it reaches room temperature.

3 Fill several small cups with this mixture and store in the refrigerator.

4 To prepare the lemon cubes, soak the gelatin in cold water. Meanwhile, heat the water, sugar, and lemon juice in a saucepan. As soon as it starts boiling, add the lemon zest and infuse for 5 minutes.

5 Strain, add the gelatin, and fill a small cubed freezer tray with the resulting mixture.

6 For the gin tonic gelatin, heat the water and sugar in a saucepan. Once hot, add the gelatin (previously hydrated in cold water and drained), tonic, and gin. Mix lightly and store in the refrigerator.

7 Add a tablespoon of gin tonic gelatin and two or three cubes of lemon in the small cups with cream.

The origin of **gin** comes from Holland. It was specifically in the seventeenth century when Franciscus Sylvius, physician and professor of medicine at the University of Leiden, sought a remedy for kidney ailments. To do this, he produced a medicinal elixir mixing alcohol from barley, corn, and rye with juniper berries. He called this new preparation *genévrier* (juniper in French). The product quickly gained popularity among soldiers and eventually became the national drink of another country: England.

AVOCADO JAM

4 servings | Difficulty: Easy

For the banana slices:
1 banana
Sugar

For the cream:
1 avocado
0.71 oz. (20 g) sugar
Juice of ½ lemon

1 Heat the oven to 340 °F (170 °C). Meanwhile, cut the banana into thin slices with the help of a mandoline.

2 Put the slices on a baking tray lined with baking paper.

3 Sprinkle the sugar on top and let bake for 35 minutes. Remove and keep in a tightly closed container.

4 For the avocado cream, mix all the ingredients together and mash with an electric mixer until a creamy texture is obtained.

5 Serve the avocado cream in between thin slices of banana.

Although they are very similar, **plantains** and **bananas** are different fruits. The banana is bigger, its skin has a bright yellow color and no spots, and its flavor is more pasty and dry. Both are high in carbohydrate content, so their caloric value is considerable. In this recipe, it is better to use banana because its fibrous texture yields crispier slices.

TAPIOCA PEARLS WITH WATERMELON, POMEGRANATE, AND ORANGE

4 servings | Difficulty: Medium

For the pearls:
0.53 oz (15 g) grenadine
  syrup
1.41 oz. (40 g) tapioca pearls
1.23 oz. (35 g) water

Other ingredients:
Watermelon
Pomegranate
Orange
Red currants

1 In a saucepan, heat the grenadine syrup, add the tapioca pearls and water, and cook for 30 minutes, stirring constantly.

2 Strain and let the pearls cool under running cold water. Set aside.

3 Dice a piece of watermelon, separate some orange slices, and a few juicy pomegranate seeds.

4 Place a few pieces of the watermelon, orange, and pomegranate seeds on a plate. Cover them with tapioca pearls and add red currants on top.

Tapioca is a white, granulated starch extracted from the cassava root.

GRILLED MELON WITH AROMATIC HERBS

4 servings | Difficulty: Medium

1 melon
Aromatic herbs

1 Cut the melon into rectangles. Take a few of the rectangles and finely dice them and store in the freezer.

2 Heat a nonstick pan and roast the remaining melon pieces on both sides. Set aside.

3 On a plate, serve the hot roasted melon, add the frozen pieces on top, and decorate with aromatic herbs.

Some good advice
Melons contain a lot of sugar in August. It will caramelize as soon as the melon is roasted in the pan, giving the dessert a more intense flavor and texture.

FRUIT CAIPIRIÑA

4 servings | Difficulty: Easy

2 gelatin sheets
10.58 oz. (300 g) water
3.53 oz. (100 g) sugar
3.53 oz. (100 g) of cachaça
 (sugar cane spirit)
Strawberries, lychees, wild
 berries, apricots, mango,
 mint leaves, and apple
Zest of 1 lime

1 Hydrate the gelatin in cold water.

2 In a saucepan heat the water and sugar. Add the gelatin.

3 Add the cachaça and keep in the refrigerator until set.

4 Wash, dry, and cut all the fruit into small cubes except for the strawberries (leave whole) and lychees (cut into quarters). Add to the gelatin (mixing well to distribute the fruit).

5 Cut the mint leaves into thin strips and grate the lime peel. Add to the gelatin, trying not to break the fruits.

6 Serve chilled in a frozen glass.

PIÑA COLADA

4 servings | Difficulty: Easy

For the pineapple:
3.53 oz. (100 g) sugar
¼ pineapple
0.88 oz. (25 g) unsalted
   butter
2.47 oz. (70 g) water
Star anise

For the coconut:
3.53 oz. (100 g) whipping
   cream
1.76 oz. (50 g) sugar
1 vanilla bean
3.53 oz. (100 g) coconut milk

1 Start with preparing the pineapple. Make a dry caramel, heating the sugar in a paella pan over low heat. As soon as it starts to color, add the pineapple (peeled and cut into quarters) and butter.

2 Dissolve the sugar by adding the water. Then add the star anise, remove from heat and let cool. Once cooled, remove the star anise.

3 Boil slowly to get a jam-like texture. Set aside.

4 For the coconut, boil the whipping cream, sugar, and vanilla seeds (which have been scraped out from the vanilla bean) in a saucepan. Remove from heat. Let it rest for a few minutes and then add the coconut milk. Let cool in the refrigerator.

5 Serve a spoonful of caramelized pineapple in cocktail glasses or small cups. With the help of an electric mixer, beat the coconut cream until it gets a foamy texture and add it on top of the pineapple.

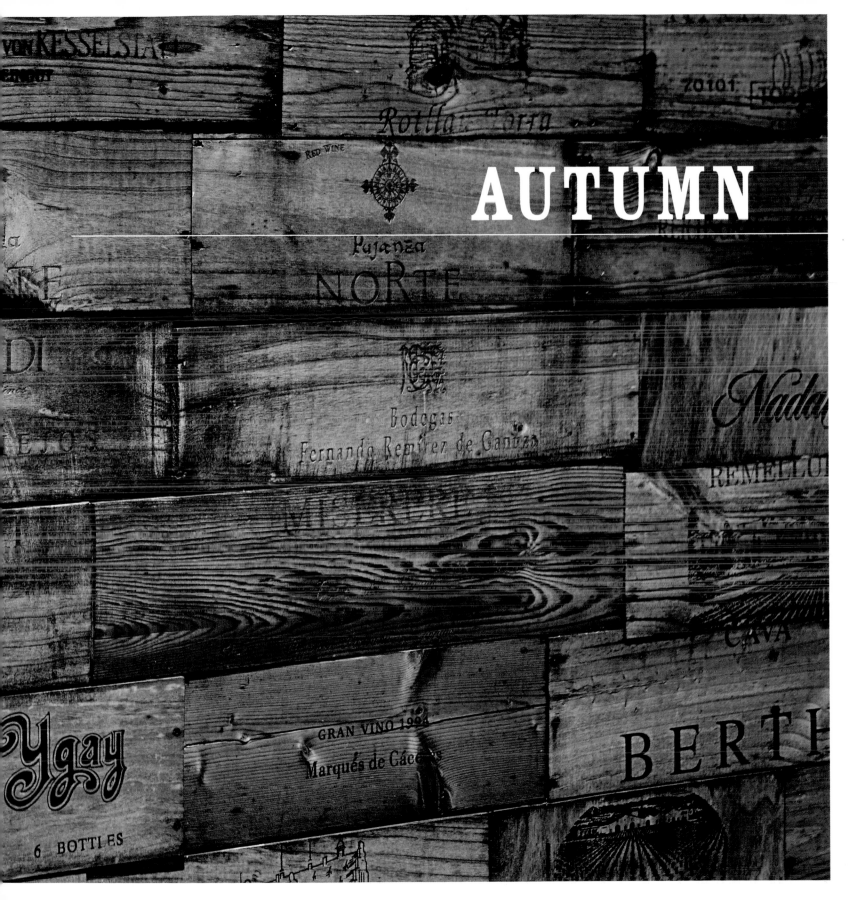

AUTUMN

CURRY AND CARROT SABAYON

4 servings | Difficulty: Easy

For the carrots:
10 to 15 baby carrots with
   stems
17.64 oz. (500 g) water
8.82 oz. (250 g) sugar

To make the sabayon:
1.76 oz. (50 g) water
3 egg yolks
5.29 oz. (150 g) sugar
A pinch of curry

1   Peel the carrots, without cutting the stems. Give them a well-rounded shape with a
    sharp knife.

2   Boil the water and sugar. Submerge the carrots carefully, trying not to wet the leaves
    to prevent them from breaking away.

3   Once blanched, cool the carrots with cold water and set aside.

4   For the sabayon, boil water in a pan. Meanwhile, mix all the other ingredients in a
    bowl and beat until very thick.

5   Put the bowl into the boiling water (using a double boiler) and continue stirring until
    the heat thickens the egg yolks and gives structure to the mixture. Once the cream is
    mixed, set aside.

6   Lastly, fill several bowls with cream. Brown using a salamander broiler at 430 °F
    (220 °C) for 1 minute, or a kitchen torch. Serve hot with carrots placed on the surface.

Note: Since this is an emulsified cream, we must increase its volume by mixing the
ingredients vigorously in a double boiler. To do so, use a wire whisk (manual or
electric) or simply use a wooden spatula.

You can add a little bit of cream or egg whites whipped to a snow-like appearance to
make it more fluffy and creamy.

You can substitute the carrots for any other fruit (apricots, cherries, strawberries, or
plums, according to the season).

A **sabayon** is a light, creamy sauce native to southern Italy, which can be served to accompany sweet
or savory dishes.

SWEET POTATO WITH
TANGERINE GRANITA

4 servings | Difficulty: Easy

For the granita:
17.64 oz. (500 g) tangerine
  juice, divided
3.53 oz. (100 g) sugar
0.71 oz. (20 g) tangerine
  liqueur, or 0.35 oz. (10 g)
  vodka

**To make the tangerine
sugar:**
1.41 oz. (40 g) tangerine skin
7.05 oz. (200 g) sugar

Other ingredients:
1 sweet potato
2 tangerines

1 Prepare the tangerine juice with the help of a juicer or blender.

2 Mix 3.53 oz. (100 g) of the juice with the sugar and heat over medium heat.

3 Once the sugar has melted completely, add the rest of the juice, then add the
   tangerine liqueur or vodka.

4 Store the mixture in a tightly sealed pie pan and set it in the freezer for a few hours,
   until it freezes completely.

5 Remove from the freezer, open the pie pan and scratch the tangerine mixture with
   a fork until it gets a granita-like texture.

6 To prepare the tangerine sugar, peel two tangerines and keep the skin. Add the skin to
   a blender along with the sugar and blend until a thick orange paste is formed.
   Set aside.

7 Heat the oven to 300 °F (150 °C) and cook the unpeeled sweet potato for about 10 to
   20 minutes, depending on the size. To test when it is perfectly cooked, you can prick
   the sweet potatoes lightly with the tip of a knife and check whether the pulp inside is
   wet or dry.

8 Cut the cooked sweet potato into irregular rectangles.

9 Serve the sweet potato pieces, some tangerine segments, several pinches of sugar,
   and a tablespoon of tangerine granita on a dessert dish.

Note: You can save the tangerine flavored sugar in a sealed container for later use.
It is perfect for burning the surface of a cream.

ORANGE WITH CANDIED BEETS
AND LICORICE GELATIN

4 servings | 40 minutes | Difficulty: Medium

To make the licorice gelatin:
10.58 oz. (300 g) water
0.71 oz. (20 g) sugar
2 sticks of licorice
0.07 oz. (2 g) agar agar

To make the beet gelatin:
7.05 oz. (200 g) beets
0.71 oz. (20 g) sugar
1 g of agar agar

Other ingredients:
1 orange
Candied beets

1 Heat the water with the sugar and licorice sticks. Bring to boil, remove from the heat, and let infuse for a few minutes.

2 Strain the infusion, add the agar agar while stirring constantly, return to boil.

3 Remove from the heat and pour into a small tray (making sure the surface is flat) and let sit at room temperature until layers of semi-thick licorice gelatin are formed.

4 Next, purée the beets, and then mix with the sugar and agar agar in a saucepan (no heat). Once mixed, turn on the heat and bring it to a boil, stirring constantly. Then remove from heat and pour into a pan deep enough to create about a 1-inch layer of gelatin. Let it sit at room temperature until set.

5 Cut the beet gelatin in squares.

6 Place a few diced candied beets on a plate, alternating with diced beet gelatin and some orange slices.

7 Finally, cover the dessert with a slice of licorice gelatin.

Agar agar is a byproduct made with different marine seaweed that is colorless, tasteless, and has high gelling power. It is capable of absorbing water in amounts of up to 300 times its own weight, forming a thick gel that does not affect the taste of the food. It can be purchased as strips, flakes, or powder, usually in 1-ounce bags (available in supermarkets). It is used in the preparation of all kinds of desserts, such as custard, mousse, cream, gelatin, and ice cream.

CANDY APPLES

4 servings | Difficulty: Medium

2 large apples
1.76 oz. (50 g) powdered
  sugar
7.05 oz. (200 g) sugar
2.12 oz. (60 g) water

1 Wash and peel the apples. Cut into small cubes.

2 Dust the cubes with powdered sugar and thread on a skewer.

3 In a small saucepan, mix the sugar and water. Cook over medium heat for 15 minutes, until it turns a caramel color.

4 Soak the apples in the caramel until they are completely covered in caramel.

5 Remove and let cool on baking paper for 5 minutes.

A good trick
Golden or Royal Gala apples are the best varieties to make this simple dessert as they contain less water.

If
you prefer . . .
You can replace the apple
with pear or any other fruit
of similar consistency.

ANGEL HAIR SQUASH

4 servings | Difficulty: Easy

1 squash 3.3 pounds (1.5 kg)
  (to yield 17.64 (500 g)
  of juice)
10.58 oz. (300 g) sugar
0.28 oz. (8 g) agar agar
Toasted pine nuts
Vanilla ice cream

1 Cut, peel, and liquefy the squash.

2 In a saucepan, mix the resulting juice with the sugar and the agar agar. Bring to a boil, stirring constantly.

3 Once boiled, pour the mixture into a large bowl and let it thicken in the fridge for 15 minutes.

4 Unmold and grate the squash gelatin to form angel hair.

5 Next put some angel hair on a soup plate, add pine nuts, and a scoop of vanilla ice cream.

Traditional **angel hair squash** is produced from a sweet winter squash, sometimes also known as Malabar gourd, fig-leaf gourd, or cidra. The winter variety is sweeter than summer squash. Its flesh is juicy, tender, and has a filament-like texture. To cook it, it is advisable to buy a squash that is as ripe as possible.

RATAFÍA GRANITA
AND COFFEE CREAM

4 servings | Difficulty: Easy

For the granita:
10.58 oz. (300 g) water
10.58 oz. (300 g) ratafía

For the cream:
10.58 oz. (300 g) whipping
  cream
1.76 oz. (50 g) sugar
1.06 oz. (30 g) coffee beans

1 Mix the water and the ratafía. Put it in a plastic pie pan and store in the freezer for at least 4 hours.

2 Remove the pan and scratch the contents with the tip of a fork until it gets the texture of a granita.

3 Next, prepare the coffee cream. In a saucepan, mix the whipping cream and sugar. Boil it and add whole coffee beans.

4 Let it infuse for 10 minutes, then strain and store in the fridge overnight.

5 The next day, whip the coffee cream until it gets a white mousse texture, but with all the aroma and flavor of coffee.

6 Fill a tall narrow cup or glass halfway with the granita and complete it with the coffee cream.

Ratafía is a liqueur distilled from a mixture of green walnuts, spices (cinnamon, nutmeg), and aromatic herbs (sage, thyme, lavender, mint). The making of ratafía is deeply rooted in Catalonia where it has held the DG seal (geographical designation) since 1989. It is an excellent liqueur to serve with cookies or dried fruits.

PEAR COMPOTE
WITH CHESTNUT CRUDITÉ

4 servings | Difficulty: Medium

For the compote:
3 pears (Conference)
3.53 oz. (100 g) sugar
1.06 oz. (30 g) unsalted
   butter
1 cinnamon stick
2 tablespoons water

To make the crudité:
3.53 oz. (100 g) raw
   chestnuts
1 pear

1   Peel and cut the pears into quarters.

2   Cook the fruit in a saucepan with the sugar, butter and cinnamon stick.

3   When the sugar begins to caramelize, add water slowly in order to slow the cooking.

4   Let it cook until the fruit is very soft.

5   In a bowl, put a spoonful of stewed pear. Cut thin slices of chestnut and raw pear with the help of a mandolin slicer and place them on top of the compote.

A good trick
You can heat the dessert in the oven just before serving and accompany with vanilla ice cream.

APPLE CREAM WITH MACADAMIA
NUTS AND CHESTNUTS

4 servings | Difficulty: Medium

For the cream:
2 Golden apples
3.53 oz. (100 g) sugar
1.76 oz. (50 g) unsalted
   butter
1 vanilla bean

Other ingredients:
Candied chestnuts
Golden apples
Macadamia nuts

1 Start by preparing the cream. Peel and cut the apples into quarters.

2 Put the fruit on a plastic pie pan. Cook in the microwave on high, together with the sugar and butter for 8 minutes.

3 Once cooked, drain the excess water, and puree the apples with the vanilla seeds (scraped from the inside of the bean) in a food processor or blender. Then store the cream in the fridge.

4 Serve the cream in a bowl and add the candied chestnuts, a few apple slices, and grated macadamia nuts.

Marrons glacés are candied chestnuts (cooked slowly with sugar and water), and are very tender and sweet. Their origins date back to ancient Greece where it was customary to preserve the fruit in jars full of honey. You can find them in supermarkets and food stores.

BANANA AND CHESTNUT CUP
WITH CHOCOLATE

4 servings | Difficulty: Medium

8 roasted chestnuts
4 bananas
2.82 oz. (80 g) sugar
0.71 oz. (20 g) unsalted
  butter
Water
0.71 oz. (20 g) rum
Milk chocolate

1   Peel and cut the chestnuts and bananas.

2   In a saucepan, heat the sugar and butter until a caramel texture is produced, and slow
    the cooking by adding a little bit of water (about 0.71 oz. [20 g], 1 tablespoon at a time)
    and rum.

3   Mix the caramel with the chestnuts and bananas. Cook until the banana is very soft.
    Remove from heat and let sit for about 5 minutes.

4   Fill a glass with caramelized bananas and chestnuts.

5   Grate chocolate on top, and serve.

A good trick
To enhance the flavor of the ingredients in the
dessert, use a 70% dark chocolate for the topping.

SWEET MANGO CHUTNEY
AND YOGURT

4 servings | Difficulty: Easy

2 ripe mangoes
3.53 oz. (100 g) sugar
0.71 oz. (20 g) balsamic
   vinegar
A pinch each of cumin,
   curry, cinnamon, nutmeg,
   cardamom, and black
   pepper
Sheep's milk yogurt

1   Peel and cut the mangoes into small pieces.

2   In a saucepan, mix the mangoes with the sugar and vinegar. Bring to a boil, remove
    from heat, and add the spices.

3   Work the mixture with a fork to break up the structure into a choppy purée.

4   Use a ring mold to place a circle of the chutney on a flat dish. Place two strips of fresh
    mango on top. Next add a dollop of sheep's milk yogurt to the plate and sprinkle with
    a bit of cinnamon, cumin, and curry.

CHOCOLATE BAR WITH CANDY

4 servings | Difficulty: Easy

3.53 oz. (100 g) 55% dark
  chocolate candy coating
8-10 candies (honey,
  eucalyptus, lemon . . .)

1 Melt the chocolate in a double boiler or in the microwave on low.

2 In a mortar, chop the candies and mix with the melted chocolate, stirring constantly.

3 Spread the mixture on a tray lined with plastic wrap and store in the refrigerator until
   it thickens completely.

4 Remove from the fridge, remove the film, cut into rectangles, and serve.

Some good advice
This soothing chocolate is great with a cup of coffee.

WHITE GRAPE COMPOTE
WITH MUSCAT WINE

4 servings | Difficulty: Easy

For the compote:
3.53 oz. (100 g) white grapes
0.71 oz. (20 g) sugar
1.76 oz. (50 g) muscat wine

For the jelly:
7.05 oz. (200 g) rose water
1 g of agar agar

Other ingredients:
2 edible roses

1 Peel and cut the grapes in half.

2 In a saucepan, mix the grapes with sugar and cook over low heat for about 10 minutes. Add the wine and remove from heat. Set aside at room temperature.

3 Boil half of the rose water with the agar agar. Remove from heat and then mix in the rest of the rose water and spread on a tray, forming a thin, ⅕ inch (½ cm) layer. Let it thicken, and cut the jelly in small ⅕ inch (½ cm) dices.

4 Fill a glass with compote halfway, add the diced rose jelly, and decorate with rose petals cut into julienne strips.

Aromatic **Muscat wine** comes from white grapes that have the same name. This variety is grown throughout the Mediterranean basin; its flavor is very sweet and musky.

WHITE GRAPE WITH MACABEO WINE

4 servings | Difficulty: Easy

7.05 oz. (200 g) white grapes
0.71 oz. (20 g) sugar
2.12 oz. (60 g) Macabeo wine
2 peaches

1   Peel and cut the grapes in half.

2   In a saucepan, mix the grapes with sugar, and cook over low heat for about 5 minutes.

3   Puree with a blender or food processor, add the wine, mix well, and strain. Store in the refrigerator.

4   Peel and cut the peaches into quarters. Store in the freezer for at least 2 hours.

5   Grate the frozen peaches with the help of a grater with a handle. Put the shredded peach back into the freezer.

6   In a bowl, add some of the grape juice and wine mixture, then a few halved grapes, and finish by sprinkling with grated peach.

The **Macabeo grape** or Viura is a white variety which is abundant in La Rioja and Catalonia. The wine made from this grape is aromatic and slightly fruity. Along with Parellada and Xarello varieties, it is used in the production of cava.

BLACK GRAPES WITH LICORICE CREAM, BLACKBERRIES, AND PEDRO XIMÉNEZ

8 servings | Difficulty: Medium

For the gelatin:
2 gelatin sheets
1.76 oz. (50 g) sugar
1.76 oz. (50 g) water
7.05 oz. (200 g)
   Pedro Ximénez wine

To make the cream:
17.64 oz. (500 g) whipping
   cream
1.76 oz. (50 g) sugar
0.35 oz. (10 g) powdered
   black licorice candy

For the infusion:
3.53 oz. (100 g) blackberries
3.53 oz. (100 g) black grapes
1.76 oz. (50 g) sugar

1 Soak the gelatin in cold water. Meanwhile, prepare a syrup with sugar and water. In a saucepan, mix and heat both ingredients. Without letting it cool, mix in the gelatin until it melts, and add the wine. Put the mixture into a plastic container, cover, and store in the fridge until it thickens completely.

2 To prepare the cream, use a beater (electric or manual) to mix the whipping cream with the sugar. Add the licorice powder, whip up the cream, and then store in the fridge.

3 To prepare the infusion, heat plenty of water in a pot. Carefully place a metal bowl containing the blackberries, grapes (peeled and cut in half) and sugar, into the water. Cover the bowl with plastic wrap and cook in a double boiler for 2 hours, on medium heat. Remove and store the infusion in the fridge.

4 Serve a little blackberry and grape infusion, Pedro Ximénez gelatin, and the whipped licorice cream in a glass.

Licorice candy (popularly known in Europe as black licorice) is made from the extract of the licorice plant, sugar, and thickeners, which give it that rubbery texture. Finely grate some licorice candy to get enough powdered black licorice candy for the recipe.

PÂTE BRISÉE WITH
SLOE SABAYON

4 servings | Difficulty: Medium

To make the pâté brisée:
4.41 oz. (125 g) sugar
3.53 oz. (100 g) unsalted butter
8.82 oz. (250 g) all-purpose flour
0.25 oz. (7 g) yeast
1 egg

To make the sabayon:
3 egg yolks
0.88 oz. (25 g) sloe brandy (Pacharán)
1.76 oz. (50 g) sugar

Other ingredients:
Sloe berries

1 Start by preparing the pâte brisée. To do this, mix the sugar and butter until it is creamy.

2 Next, mix and sift the flour and yeast. Add the dry ingredients to the creamed butter and sugar, continue mixing, and add the egg. Work it until you get a thin dough.

3 Stretch the dough and cut it into about 3-inch diameter discs.

4 Place the dough into silicone tartlet molds and put it in the oven at 390 °F (200 °C) for 10 minutes.

5 Remove from the molds and set aside.

6 Continue with the sabayon. In a metal bowl, mix all ingredients. While stirring constantly, place the bowl over a flame so that the contents mix and double in volume.

7 Fill the tart with sloe berries, cover with sabayon, and lightly brown with a kitchen torch.

The **Pâte brisée**, or flaky dough, is widely used in the preparation of sweet and savory tarts. It is characterized by its soft and crispy texture.

If
you prefer . . .
You can substitute
the sloe berries for
any other fruit and its
corresponding spirits
(raspberry, plum,
cherry, pear) to
make the sabayon.

WINTER

TRUFFLE CUPCAKES

8 servings | Difficulty: Easy

7.05 oz. (200 g) unsalted
   butter
8.64 oz. (245 g) all-purpose
   flour
4.23 oz. (120 g) powdered
   sugar
0.35 oz. (10 g) baking
   powder
5 eggs
3.53 oz. (100 g) honey
3.53 oz. (100 g) canned
   truffles, chopped
Pinch of salt

1   Melt butter in a saucepan over medium heat or place in the microwave for a couple of minutes. Set aside.

2   Mix and sift the flour together with the powdered sugar and baking powder.

3   Beat the eggs with the honey, chopped truffles, and salt.

4   Add the butter to the egg mixture and stir constantly. Then add the flour and sugar mixture and combine.

5   Let it stand overnight in the refrigerator.

6   Line several cupcake pans with paper baking cups and fill with the batter. Bake in the oven at 375 °F (190 °C) for approximately 8 minutes.

A good trick
In order for the cupcakes to have a more intense flavor a teaspoon of truffle oil can be added, available in stores selling gourmet products.

CITRUS AND ORANGE BLOSSOM MADELEINES

8 servings | Difficulty: Easy

6.35 oz. (180 g) unsalted butter
8.29 oz. (235 g) all-purpose flour
4.94 oz. (140 g) powdered sugar
0.28 oz. (8 g) baking powder
5 eggs
3.53 oz. (100 g) milk
1.76 oz. (50 g) honey
0.71 oz. (20 g) orange blossom water
Pinch of salt
Orange zest

1 Melt the butter in a saucepan over medium heat or place it in the microwave for a few minutes. Set aside.

2 Mix and sift together the flour, powdered sugar, and baking powder.

3 Mix the eggs with the milk, honey, orange blossom water, salt, and orange zest.

4 Add the melted butter to the egg mixture and stir constantly. Then add the mixture of flour, sugar, and baking powder, and combine.

5 Let it stand overnight in the refrigerator.

6 Pour the batter into several shell-shaped molds and bake in the oven at 375 °F (190 °C) for approximately 5 minutes.

A good trick
To further enhance the flavor of the madeleines, sprinkle with grated orange peel just before placing them in the oven.

CURRY CUPCAKES
WITH RED FRUIT

8 servings | Difficulty: Easy

7.05 oz. (200 g) unsalted butter
8.64 oz. (245 g) all-purpose flour
5.29 oz. (150 g) powdered sugar
0.35 oz. (10 g) baking powder
5 eggs
3.53 oz. (100 g) honey
3.53 oz. (100 g) milk
A pinch of curry
Red fruits (sloes, red currants, raspberries)

1   Melt butter in a saucepan over medium heat or place in the microwave for a couple of minutes. Set aside.

2   Mix and sift together the flour, powdered sugar, and baking powder.

3   Meanwhile, mix the eggs with the honey.

4   Heat the milk and curry. Let it cool slightly and mix in the melted butter, then add to the egg mixture.

5   Stirring constantly, add the mixture of flour, sugar, and baking soda.

6   Let stand overnight in refrigerator.

7   Using a pastry bag, distribute the batter into several silicone molds.

8   Add two or three pieces of red fruit to each mold.

9   Bake in the oven at 375 °F (190 °C) for approximately 5 minutes.

GIANT COOKIE

8 servings | Difficulty: Easy

4.41 oz. (125 g) unsalted
  butter
5.29 oz. (150 g) sugar
5.29 oz. (150 g) cane/raw
  sugar
5 eggs
12 oz. (340 g) all-purpose
  flour, sifted
0.11 oz. (3 g) baking soda
0.07 oz. (2 g) vanilla extract
5.29 oz. (150 g) dark
  chocolate, chopped
Nuts

1   Leave the butter at room temperature for half an hour before starting.

2   Using a mixer, mix the butter with the two types of sugar.

3   Mix in the eggs one by one, then add the sifted flour with the baking soda, vanilla aroma, and finally, chocolate chips and nuts.

4   Form a large ball with the dough and flatten on a baking tray lined with parchment paper.

5   Stretch the dough to make a giant cookie, about 1 inch thick and as wide as the tray allows.

6   Heat the oven to 350 °F (180 °C) and bake the cookie for 15 minutes. It should become soft and slightly golden brown.

Note: The preparation of this recipe is for making cookies of any size. The only thing to consider is the cooking time and temperature. The smaller the size, the less time cookies need to bake, with a higher temperature (approximately 8 minutes at 390° F [200 °C]).

Softened butter is a term widely used in baking. It refers to butter at room temperature that is ideal to work with. It is softer than when stored in the refrigerator.

You can buy rolls of **parchment paper** in different sizes for preparing your recipes. They are usually sold in specialty cookware stores. Alternatively you can use aluminum foil, which is an excellent transmitter of heat, but food sticks to it more easily.

THE GREAT CUPCAKE

8 servings | Difficulty: Medium

For the cupcake batter:
7.05 oz. (200 g) sugar
4.94 oz. (140 g) unsalted
  butter
2 eggs (at room
  temperature)
8.11 oz. (230 g) all-purpose
  flour
0.21 oz. (6 g) baking powder
Pinch of salt
5.29 oz. (150 g) milk
½ vanilla bean

For the frosting:
5.29 oz. (150 g) unsalted
  butter
7.05 oz. (200 g) powdered
  sugar
½ vanilla bean
Blackberries, raspberries,
  strawberries

1   Start with the cupcake batter. Using an electric mixer, combine the sugar with the butter until it becomes a fluffy cream.

2   Add the eggs one by one until they are fully combined into the mixture.

3   In another bowl, mix the flour, baking powder, and salt.

4   Separately mix the milk and vanilla seeds that have been scraped out of the bean.

5   Add the flour mixture to the initial mixture of butter, sugar, and eggs.

6   Add the milk with vanilla, and mix well until it becomes creamy, thick, and homogeneous.

7   Coat a large pan with butter and fill it with the batter. It is important to leave a space of about 1.5 inches (4 cm) below the top edge of the mold.

8   Bake at 340 °F (170 °C) for 25 minutes.

9   To prepare the frosting, put the softened butter (at room temperature) in a bowl with the sugar and vanilla seeds that have been scraped out of the bean. Whip the mixture until it takes on a whitish tone with a creamy texture.

10 Put the frosting in a pastry bag with a curly tip.

11 Once the cupcake has baked, let it cool completely and pipe the frosting on it. Then place berries on top.

Note: Before removing the cupcake from the oven, make sure it is perfectly baked. To do this, prick it with the tip of a knife. If the knife is slightly damp it means that there are still a few more minutes of cooking left.

This recipe is inspired by the classic American "**cupcake**." It appeared in the early nineteenth century when pastry molds did not exist and instead small individual bowls or clay stewing pots were used. This gave rise to the name "cup" and "cake."

LARGE CHOCOLATE AND HAZELNUT BONBON

8 servings | Difficulty: Very high

For the candies:
8.82 oz. (250 g) chocolate fondant
4.41 oz. (125 g) glucose
4.41 oz. (125 g) isomalt sugar
10 drops of citric acid in a 50% solution

For the mousse:
3.53 oz. (100 g) sugar
17.64 oz. (½ kg) whipping cream
3 egg yolks
5.29 oz. (150 g) 70% baking chocolate
2 gelatin sheets

For the praline cream:
7.05 oz. (200 g) whipping cream
8.82 oz. (250 g) hazelnut praline paste

For the chocolate sauce:
11.29 oz. (320 g) whipping cream
19.75 oz. (560 g) water
28.22 oz. (800 g) sugar
11.29 oz. (320 g) cocoa powder

For the chocolate coating:
10.58 oz. (300 g) 70% baking chocolate
10.58 oz. (300 g) cocoa butter

1   Start by preparing the candies. In a saucepan, cook the fondant, glucose, and isomalt sugar until 300 °F (150 °C) is reached. Add the citric acid and raise the temperature to 325 °F (160 °C).

2   Roll out the mixture on a Silpat and knead back and forth 20 times.

3   Cut balls of ½ inch (1 cm) in diameter and, with a pump, blow air into the interior to form small spherical bubbles. Cut the end that connects the pump to the candy and set aside in a dry place.*

4   Start preparing the mousse by heating the sugar in a small saucepan. Stir the whipping cream and yolks into the saucepan until it reaches a temperature of 185 °F (85 °C). Remove from heat and add the chocolate and gelatin. Pour into an electric blender, blend, and then strain. Let it stand in the refrigerator for at least 12 hours. Then, put it into a whipping siphon (*see page 56*).

5   For the praline cream, heat the whipping cream in a saucepan until it reaches a boil. When it comes to a boil, add the hazelnut praline paste and whisk until it becomes smooth and glossy. Remove from heat and set aside.

6   For the chocolate sauce, mix the whipping cream, water, and sugar in a saucepan over high heat. Once it comes to a boil, remove from heat and mix in the cocoa powder with an electric mixer. Strain and store in the refrigerator until needed.

7   For the chocolate coating, melt the baking chocolate and cocoa butter over low heat and mix together. Then coat the candy balls (from step #3) in the chocolate, stuff them with chocolate mousse (using a whipping cream siphon) and place them on a plate over a base of chocolate sauce and praline cream.

*We use a pump with a non-return valve attached to a silicone tube and a cylinder of metal (usually steel). The metal tube is where we stick the sphere of solid candy, and blowing with the pump, inflate it until it reaches the correct density. To take the sphere off of the metal tube, use a kitchen torch. Quickly heat a metal ring with the torch to sink in the area and make the hole where the sphere will be filled later.

SUGARED TANGERINES

4 servings | Difficulty: Easy

2 tangerines
1 gelatin sheet
1 egg white
Sugar
Basil

1 Peel and separate the tangerine segments, being careful not to break the thin membrane that protects them.

2 Distribute the segments on a plate or tray and keep at room temperature until the following day so that they are able to dry.

3 Soak the gelatin sheet in cold water and while it becomes saturated, leave the egg white at room temperature in a bowl.

4 Drain the gelatin and place it in a plastic container in the microwave. Heat it at the maximum temperature until it breaks up, and without letting it cool, mix with the egg white while stirring constantly.

5 Coat the tangerine segments, one by one, in the gelatin.

6 Drain the segments on absorbent paper and then dip them in sugar.

7 Place the segments on a drying rack and leave them to dry on both sides for 2 to 3 hours.

8 Place sugared tangerines in a serving cup and add a few basil leaves.

Only with tangerines
This dessert can only be done with this type of citrus since oranges, lemons, and grapefruits do not have a solid enough membrane to be handled without breaking.

GRAPEFRUIT WITH GINGER

8 servings | Difficulty: Medium

For the ginger cream:
2 gelatin sheets
17.64 oz. (½ kg) whipping
  cream
1.76 oz. (50 g) sugar
0.02 oz. (0.5 g) powdered
  ginger

For the jam:
2 grapefruits
7.05 oz. (200 g) sugar

Other ingredients:
Grapefruit
Candied ginger

1. Start by preparing the ginger cream. Soak the gelatin in cold water, while heating the whipping cream and sugar in a small saucepan. Bring to a boil, remove from heat, and add the drained gelatin and powdered ginger. Let stand for 5 minutes, strain the mixture, and store in the refrigerator. It is best to prepare the cream the day before or at least a few hours before.

2. Once cold and set, beat the ginger cream until its texture is like that of whipped cream.

3. Fill several bowls three-quarters full of the cream, which will be the dessert base.

4. To prepare the jam, peel and cut the grapefruits in quarters and liquefy them.

5. Weigh the resulting juice and add the same weight in sugar (should be about 7.05 oz [200g]). Heat and reduce the mixture in a small saucepan over low heat until the desired texture is achieved.

6. Cut several slices of grapefruit and dice some candied ginger. Put them on top of the whipped cream and cover with the grapefruit jam.

The sweet, spicy, and slightly bitter flavor of **ginger** comes from a substance called gingerol that is present in the root of the plant. We suggest using just enough, as it is very intense and can mask the taste of other ingredients.

A good trick

So that the cream can whip up quickly, let it cool in the refrigerator for 30 minutes before using it.

LIME MOUSSE AND MAPLE SYRUP

4 servings | Difficulty: Medium

For the mousse:
7.05 oz. (200 g) whipping
   cream
3 gelatin sheets
5 egg whites
2.65 oz. (75 g) sugar
Zest of 1 lemon

Other ingredients:
Maple syrup
Mint leaves

1   Whip the whipping cream with a wire whisk and then store in the refrigerator.

2   Saturate the gelatin sheets by soaking them in cold water. Meanwhile, mix the egg whites and sugar in a bowl. Cook the mixture in a double boiler (at a temperature of 122 °F [50 °C]) so that the sugar dissolves but the egg whites do not cook.

3   Whip the still warm egg white and sugar mixture until it obtains a white and consistent texture. This can be done by hand or with a mixer. Add the lemon zest.

4   With a spatula, mix in the cooled whipped cream from the refrigerator.

5   Spread the resulting mousse into a rectangular mold, lined with parchment paper to simplify its removal.

6   Let the mousse set in the refrigerator for a couple of hours.

7   Unmold and cut in uniform cubes (the gelatin will keep the shape without breaking).

8   Fill several cups or bowls with a little maple syrup, add three or four mousse cubes, and finally garnish with mint leaves.

Maple syrup is a sweet syrup made from the sap of the maple tree. The use of this ingredient is very common in American and Canadian cuisine, mostly as a garnish or complement to waffles, pancakes, and toast.

CHOCOLATE AND
RASPBERRY BRANDY BONBON

8 servings | Difficulty: Medium

10.58 oz. (300 g) whipping cream
2.82 oz. (80 g) honey
26.46 oz. (750 g) milk chocolate
3.53 oz. (100 g) dark chocolate
3.53 oz. (100 g) raspberry brandy
5.29 oz. (150 g) unsalted butter
35.27 oz. (1 kg) 70% dark chocolate candy coating
3.53 oz. (100 g) cocoa powder

1 In a saucepan boil the whipping cream and honey.

2 Place the two chocolates in a bowl, and add the boiling cream, stirring constantly.

3 Add the brandy and continue stirring until a very fine texture is achieved.

4 Add the butter cut into cubes and stir until the mixture is well blended.

5 Pour the mixture into a pan lined with parchment paper and let sit in the refrigerator for at least 8 hours.

6 Cut square pieces of the resulting dough and knead by hand into a spherical shape. Melt the dark chocolate candy coating in a microwave on low. Coat the balls with the melted chocolate. Finally, sprinkle with cocoa powder.

ORANGE BLOSSOM BONBON

4 servings | Difficulty: Medium

6.53 oz. (185 g) whipping
  cream
3.17 oz. (90 g) honey
54.68 oz. (1550 g) milk
  chocolate candy coating,
  divided
2.65 oz. (75 g) unsalted
  butter
0.71 oz. (40 g) orange
  blossom water
3.53 oz. (100 g) cocoa
  powder

1 In a saucepan boil the whipping cream and honey.

2 Meanwhile, fill the electric mixer bowl with about 19.40 oz. (550 g) of the milk
   chocolate candy coating.

3 Add the boiling cream mixture, and mix at low speed until the chocolate is melted.

4 Add the softened butter and orange water. Continue beating until it is well blended.

5 Pour the mixture into a tray and store in the refrigerator to set for a minimum of
   6 hours.

6 Cut into squares of preferred size and knead each into a round shape.

7 Melt the remaining milk chocolate candy coating and coat the balls with the
   chocolate. Let cool and coat with cocoa powder.

If
you prefer . . .
You can substitute
the orange infused
water with an infusion
of aromatic herbs.

COCONUT AND YOGURT BONBON

4 servings | Difficulty: Medium

7.05 oz. (200 g) Greek yogurt
1.76 oz. (50 g) honey
3.53 oz. (100 g) grated
  coconut, divided
14.11 oz. (400 g) white
  chocolate candy coating
1.76 oz. (50 g) powdered milk

1   In a bowl, mix the yogurt, honey, and 1.76 oz. (50 g) of the grated coconut. It is
    important that the ingredients be at room temperature.

2   Stirring constantly, melt the chocolate candy coating in the microwave and then add
    to the yogurt mixture and combine.

3   Spread the mixture out on a tray and put in the refrigerator for a couple of hours until
    it sets.

4   Cut into squares of preferred size and knead each into a round shape.

5   Coat the balls with the remaining grated coconut and powdered milk.

CHOCOLATE GINGER COOKIES

8 servings | Difficulty: Easy

2.65 oz. (75 g) unsalted butter
3.53 oz. (100 g) raw sugar
2.65 oz. (75 g) sugar
1 egg
0.35 oz. (10 g) vanilla extract
7.05 oz. (200 g) all-purpose flour
1.06 oz. (30 g) cornstarch
0.35 oz. (10 g) baking soda
Pinch of salt
3.53 oz. (100 g) chopped chocolate, milk or dark
Diced candied ginger

1 Take the butter out of the refrigerator and leave it standing at room temperature until soft.

2 In a large bowl, mix the sugars and softened butter by hand. Then mix in the egg and vanilla extract.

3 Sift the flour together with the cornstarch and baking soda. Stirring constantly, gradually add into the butter and sugar mixture. Finish by adding the salt and half of the chopped chocolate. Let it stand a few minutes in the refrigerator.

4 Cover an oven tray with parchment paper. Form several balls with the stored dough and flatten slightly to form cookies. Distribute the remaining chopped chocolate over the tops along with the candied ginger.

5 Bake the cookies at 350 °F (180 °C) for 7 minutes.

A good trick
These cookies are much tastier when they are freshly made. They can be served with vanilla ice cream on top.

SABLÉ COOKIES

8 servings | Difficulty: Easy

7.05 oz. (200 g) unsalted
   butter
7.94 oz. (225 g) all-purpose
   flour
1.76 oz. (50 g) powdered
   sugar
1 egg yolk
Arugula sprouts

1   Soften the butter and knead by hand in a large bowl.

2   Sift the flour with the powdered sugar, and then add the butter.

3   While stirring continually, add the egg yolk and let it stand a few minutes in the refrigerator.

4   Cover a baking tray with parchment paper. Form several balls with the dough and lightly flatten them to make cookies.

5   Bake at 350 °F (180 °C) for 5 minutes (depending on size).

6   Remove from the oven, and carefully make holes in the center of the cookies for the arugula sprouts.

Sablé (sandy, in French) is a dry, crisp cookie originally from Caen, in the French province of Normandy. Its name comes from its characteristic texture that resembles the sand on the beach.

COCOA COOKIES

8 servings | Difficulty: Easy

7.05 oz. (200 g) unsalted
  butter
7.05 oz. (200 g) all-purpose
  flour
1.76 oz. (50 g) powdered
  sugar
1.06 oz. (30 g) of cocoa
Pinch of salt
1 egg
Ice cream (optional)

1   Soften the butter and knead by hand in a large bowl.

2   Sift the flour with the powdered sugar, cocoa, and salt, and then mix in the butter.

3   Stirring continuously, add the egg and let stand a few minutes in the freezer.

4   Spread the dough between two sheets of parchment paper to a thickness of about 1/8 inch (3mm), and let it stand in the freezer for 20 minutes.

5   With a round dough-cutter cut several circles of dough.

6   Place the circles of dough on a baking tray covered with parchment paper. Bake at 350 °F (180 °C) for 5 minutes.

7   If you want to create ice cream cookie sandwiches, use a round cookie cutter to cut several cylinders of ice cream and place the ice cream in between two cookies.

If you prefer . . .
The cocoa cookies can be filled with chocolate truffle, bitter orange jam, or any other cream mentioned in this book.

WHITE CHOCOLATE, TOASTED COCONUT, AND CURRY BARK

8 servings | Difficulty: Medium

7.05 oz. (200 g) of white chocolate
2.65 oz. (75 g) shredded coconut
Zest of ½ lemon
A pinch of curry

1 Melt the chocolate in a double boiler, or in the microwave on low. Set aside.

2 Meanwhile, spread the shredded coconut on a baking tray and toast it lightly in the oven at a low temperature.

3 Sprinkle the toasted coconut over the chocolate and add the zest of ½ lemon.

4 Stirring constantly, add the curry.

5 Cover a tray with parchment paper and pour in the chocolate coconut mixture. Leave it to cool.

6 Cut the solid piece with a sharp knife or simply break by hand, creating irregular shapes.

CRUNCHY CORN BAR

8 servings | Difficulty: Medium

3.53 oz. (100 g) unsalted
  butter
14.11 oz. (400 g) chocolate
  (55% cocoa)
5.29 oz. (150 g) roasted corn
1.76 oz. (50 g) olive oil
1.06 oz. (30 g) cocoa powder

1 Remove the butter from the refrigerator to soften.

2 Meanwhile, melt the chocolate in a double boiler or microwave on low.

3 In a mortar or with a food processor, lightly chop the roasted corn.

4 Mix the melted chocolate with the olive oil and let it cool until it reaches a temperature of 95 °F (35 °C).

5 Add the butter and, stirring constantly, add the roasted corn.

6 Spread the mixture into a pan (or mold) which has been lined with parchment paper. Place it in the refrigerator and let it solidify.

7 Cut or remove from molds. Coat with cocoa powder and serve the dish decorated with roasted corn.

A good trick
The corn can be replaced by another nut, previously candied to give more of a crunch to the bar.

LIME MERINGUE

4 servings | Difficulty: Easy

2 egg whites
Pinch of salt
2.65 oz. (75 g) sugar
Zest of 2 limes

1 Mix the egg whites and salt with a wire whisk (manual or electric).

2 When they start to get a whitish hue, slowly add the sugar.

3 Continue to blend the mixture until it turns into a thick meringue.

4 Add the lime zest and mix well, until the meringue takes on a slightly greenish hue.

5 Fill a pastry bag with meringue and use a plain nozzle of 1 inch (2 cm) in diameter.

6 Squeeze several swirls of meringue onto a cookie sheet lined with parchment paper.

7 Put in the oven at low temperature (140-190 °F [60-90 °C]) for 3 hours.

8 Once the meringues dry, they can be kept in a sealed plastic container.

A good trick
This simple recipe can be prepared as a crunchy complement to a sorbet or ice cream or to accompany a cake or a sweet snack to have with coffee.

SPICED MERINGUE

4 servings | Difficulty: Easy

For the meringue:
2 egg whites
Pinch of salt
2.65 oz. (75 g) sugar
1 tablespoon of spices (use
   a variety of spices to
   make up the 1 tablespoon,
   such as cinnamon, anise,
   turmeric, and coriander)

For the spice mix:
1 part ground cinnamon
½ part anise powder
¼ part turmeric
¼ part coriander

1   Mix the egg whites and salt with a wire whisk (manual or electric).

2   When they start to get a whitish hue, slowly add the sugar.

3   Continue to blend the mixture until it turns into a thick meringue.

4   Add the desired variety and amount of spices.

5   Put a small part of the mixture inside of a plastic mold in the form of a long leaf.
    Unmold the meringue (from the leaf mold) and repeat until you have used up all of
    the mixture.

6   Put several shaped meringues on a cookie sheet lined with parchment paper.

7   Bake at 175 °F (80 °C) for 3 hours.

8   Once the meringue leaves are dried, increase the temperature to 248 °F (120 °C)
    so they can increase in size.

9   For the spice mix, combine the spices in a bowl and then coat the meringues with the
    mixture.

10 Serve, or store in an airtight plastic container.

MINT MERINGUE

4 servings | Difficulty: Easy

2 egg whites
2.82 oz. (80 g) sugar
1.76 oz. (50 g) mint syrup
Fresh mint leaves (optional)
Pink pepper (optional)

1 Mix the egg whites with a wire whisk (manual or electric).

2 In a saucepan, cook the sugar and mint syrup over medium heat. Let it boil for a few minutes until it is visibly reduced.

3 Gradually add the hot sugar to the egg whites and continue blending the mix. Let cool.

4 Fill a pastry bag with the mixture, and apply several swirls of meringue onto a baking tray lined with parchment paper. Using a spatula, form small, elongated leaves.

5 Bake at 176 °F (80 °C) for 3 hours and serve.

Note: This meringue can be kept in an airtight plastic container to be used in other desserts.

The meringue can be served interspersed with fresh mint leaves.

The grains of pink pepper form an interesting combination with this type of meringue.

DARK CHOCOLATE AND BANANA CAKE WITH LIME

4 servings | Difficulty: Medium

For the batter:
4 egg yolks
5.64 oz. (160 g) sugar
5.29 oz. (150 g) unsalted butter
7.94 oz. (225 g) all-purpose flour
1.06 oz. (30 g) cocoa powder
0.53 oz. (15 g) baking powder
3 ripe bananas, sliced
3.53 oz. (100 g) 50% dark chocolate, chopped

For the sautéd bananas:
3.53 oz. (50 g) sugar
2 bananas, sliced
A splash of rum
Zest of 1 lime

1   Using a wire whisk, mix the egg yolks with the sugar and add the softened butter. Mix well and add the flour, cocoa, and baking powder, (previously mixed and sifted).

2   Prepare a circular sponge cake mold. If the mold is made of silicone, it will be enough to coat it lightly with butter so the cake will not stick. If it's made of metal, it will need to be buttered with flour spread over the entire surface.

3   Once the mold is ready, pour in the batter and scatter in the bananas.

4   Add the chopped chocolate on top to melt during cooking.

5   Bake at 350 °F (180 °C) for 15 minutes. Let cool to room temperature.

6   For the sautéd bananas, make a caramel by cooking the sugar at low heat in a saucepan. Add the sliced bananas and cook a few more minutes.

7   Slow the cooking by pouring in the rum, and remove from heat.

8   Put caramelized banana slices on top of the cake and sprinkle with lime zest.

PEARS IN WINE TART

4 servings | Difficulty: Medium

3.53 oz. (100 g) sugar
2.47 oz. (70 g) almond
   flour
0.71 oz. (20 g) all-purpose
   flour
5.29 oz. (150 g) whipping
   cream
3.53 oz. (100 g) red wine
5 eggs
3 egg yolks
4 pears (Conference)
1.76 oz. (50 g) powdered
   sugar
Cinnamon ice cream
   (optional)

1   Sift together the sugar, almond flour, and flour.

2   Gently mix in the whipping cream, red wine, eggs, and egg yolks. If necessary, an
    electric mixer can be used. Let sit overnight.

3   Coat 4 individual molds (4 to 5 inches [10 to 12 cm] in diameter) with butter and flour.
    Pour the batter into the molds.

4   Peel and cut the pears into slices and place on top of the tarts. Sprinkle with powdered
    sugar.

5   Bake for 10-12 minutes at 356-374 °F (180-190 °C). Unmold the cakes and store them at
    room temperature.

6   Before serving, the tarts can be warmed slightly, and topped with cinnamon ice cream
    (optional).

If you prefer . . .
Other fruits of similar consistency can be used as a substitute for the pears.

HOT WHITE CHOCOLATE CAKE WITH RASPBERRIES

4 servings | Difficulty: Easy

3.53 oz. (100 g) unsalted
  butter
8.82 oz. (250 g) white
  chocolate
3 egg yolks
4 or 5 egg whites,
  depending on size
3.53 oz. (50 g) sugar
Raspberries
Pistachios
Powdered sugar

1 Melt the butter and white chocolate in a saucepan.

2 Add the egg yolks, stirring constantly. Remove from heat and set aside.

3 Prepare a meringue by whisking the egg whites until they start to get a whitish hue, then slowly add the sugar. Continue to whisk until it turns into a thick meringue. Slowly fold in the mixture of butter, chocolate, and egg yolks, trying to prevent the meringue from losing its volume.

4 Butter the molds for the tarts and sprinkle with flour. Fill the molds and bake at a temperature of 355 °F (180 °C) for 15 minutes.

5 When ready, remove the molds from oven, let them cool slightly, and garnish with whole raspberries, pistachios, and powdered sugar.

Recipe List
by Theme

Alphabetical Recipe List

Other Recommended Books (in Spanish)

– *La Cocina al Vacío* (Sous-vide Cooking), by Joan Roca and Salvador Brugués. Montagud Editores, Barcelona, 2003.
– *La Cuina de la Meva Mare* (My Mother's Kitchen), by Joan Roca. Columna Edicions, Barcelona, 2004.
– *El Celler de Can Roca, una simfonia fantàstica* (a fantastic symphony), by Jaume Coll. Montagud Publishers, 2006.
– *Dolces sensacions* (Sweet Sensations), by Jordi Roca. Ara Llibres, Barcelona, 2007.
– *Deu menús per a concert* (Ten Menus for a concert) by Joan Roca. Galerata, Barcelona, 2008.
– *Vins compartits* (Shared Wines), by Marcel Gorgori and Josep Roca. Columna Edicions, Barcelona, 2009.